ON THE SHOULDERS OF GIANTS

LEARNING LEADERSHIP SKILLS FROM GREAT AMERICANS

On the Shoulders of Giants

Learning Leadership Skills from Great Americans

Richard L. Godfrey
Hyrum W. Smith
and
Gerreld L. Pulsipher

Hegemony Press
An Imprint of Cedar Fort, Inc.
Springville, Utah

ISBN 13: 978-1-59955-926-1

Published by Hegemony Press, an imprint of Cedar Fort, Inc., 2373 W. 700 S., Springville, UT 84663
Distributed by Cedar Fort, Inc., www.cedarfort.com

LIBRARY OF CONGRESS CATALOGING-IN-PUBLICATION DATA

Godfrey, Richard L. (Richard Lorin), 1958-, author.
On the shoulders of giants : learning leadership skills from great Americans / Richard L. Godfrey, Hyrum W. Smith.
p. cm.
Includes bibliographical references.
ISBN 978-1-59955-926-1
1. United States--History. 2. Leadership--United States. I. Smith, Hyrum W., author. II. Title.
E178.G63 2011
973--dc23

2011030947

Cover design by Brian Halley
Cover design © 2011 by Lyle Mortimer
Edited and typeset by Kelley Konzak

Printed in the United States of America

10 9 8 7 6 5 4 3 2 1

Printed on acid-free paper

PRAISE FOR

ON THE SHOULDERS OF GIANTS

[The authors] teach us through terrific stories of common folks and prominent citizens who overcame severe adversity to make a lasting impact on history, mankind, and our world. They do this with meticulous descriptions of the setting, times, and related events, drawing readers into a virtual reality experience. Extracting crucial principles for meeting today's myriad challenges, they then inspire us with hope and optimism for a more rewarding and meaningful life.

DR. LARRY D. DAUGHERTY
Superintendent, Eastern Kansas Christian Schools, Inc.

[On the Shoulders of Giants] *is the right message at the right time, just what our country needs! [The authors] have reminded us, through a series of interesting stories, how much attitude matters. Adversity is always present; those who make a difference are able to manage through and overcome tough times. A great read for every American.*

JULIA STEWART
Chairman of the Board, IHOP Corporation

Maybe the best test of the book's potential is the reader's answer to the question, "Is this a book I would want my own children to read, study, and discuss?" In my case, the answer is an unequivocal "yes." . . . The necessity for bravery in the face of ignorance and oppression is among the eternal verities that I would want my children to understand and embrace. This book is a blueprint for how to do that successfully.

TIM HEGSTROM
Dean, College of Social Sciences
San Jose State University

This is the perfect book for our uncertain times. Our country has been able to rise to the occasion time after time to retain its position as a world leader. Thanks . . . for reminding us that we can do it again.

KEN BLANCHARD
Coauthor of *The One Minute Manager* and *Leading at a Higher Level*

MORE PRAISE FOR

ON THE SHOULDERS OF GIANTS

[The authors] powerfully capture the strength of our unrelenting American spirit of courage, innovation, and a never quit certainty that we can conquer the challenges surrounding us. Inspiring, optimistic, and timely, [On the Shoulders of Giants] *is a cultural keystone reminding us that high trust, accountability, and effective leadership can move mountains, stanch floods, and help us grow forward—as individual leaders and a nation united for positive change.*

STEPHEN M. R. COVEY
Author of *The New York Times* bestseller *The Speed of Trust*

It is through insightful knowledge and personal experiences that the authors are able to relate the struggles and triumphs of our American heroes. This book serves as an inspirational education in determination and perseverance. [The authors] are great Americans and have performed a grand service to our nation by devoting time and expertise to the completion of this most excellent historical piece.

MASTER SGT. MARK "RANGER" JONES (US ARMY RET.)
Founder of The Ranger Group, a service-disabled, veteran-owned construction technology company

---

America's history is painted with detail throughout this book. Each story builds on the one before, as the reader gets a taste of what our forefathers went through, and [On the Shoulders of Giants] *shows how we are a part of this same legacy. As you read and devour the details of how our nation was built and how Americans have faced many challenging times, you will realize, as I did, that we can successfully confront challenging times that loom ahead. This is a nation that was built by "the Brave" and still lives on by "the Brave." This is who we are.*

SERGEANT JILL STEVENS
US Army Combat Medic and Miss Utah 2007

MORE PRAISE FOR

ON THE SHOULDERS OF GIANTS

This is a book that every American should read. I would especially recommend it to all members of Congress, as a reminder of who we are and how we deal with challenging times.

JAKE GARN
Former US Senator and Astronaut

Confronting today's challenging times and waves of global crises demands consistent and capable leadership . . . leaders who are not only agile and adaptive to the complexities of our interconnected world, but also leaders who can think critically and creatively while maintaining balance in their lives. Drawing examples from several of America's great pillars of leadership, [On the Shoulders of Giants] *superbly reinforces the vital role of servant leadership during some of our nation's most trying times, and inspires us to look to our past when facing the uncertainties of the future.*

LT. GENERAL WILLIAM CALDWELL
US Army

This book inspires you with courage, confidence and the determination to face and overcome every obstacle on your journey to a great life.

BRIAN TRACY
Author of *How Leaders Lead*

Affecting the human gut is the best way storytellers can inspire and breathe hope into people facing emotional and financial crises. . . .The historic stories [the authors] tell are tied into lessons designed to help "you think yourself through situations where you have little control." . . . What makes this book different from other self-help publications . . . is the use of stories from U.S. history.

SALT LAKE TRIBUNE

For Heather, Gail, and Nancy
Without whom we are nothing

CONTENTS

ACKNOWLEDGMENTS

A great editor has at least three talents: the skill to edit, the courage to be honest, and the humility to be flexible. We have found all three of these talents in Terra Davis. Terra helped us edit both *On the Shoulders of Giants* and *The Seven Laws of Learning*. Where you find simplicity and clarity, it is her doing. The muddiness and occasional confusion are all ours.

Jon Rowberry, a man unfettered by ego, always willing to do the least and the greatest of tasks, brought our efforts out of chaos and into clarity. As always, he turned nonsense into sense.

Although all of us contributed to the content of the book, we chose to speak through Richard's voice. Many of the examples and stories come from his experience, and a single narrator, we believe, results in a stronger and more understandable message.

— Richard L. Godfrey
— Hyrum W. Smith
— Gerreld L. Pulsipher

Oh, say can you see by the dawn's early light

What so proudly we hailed at the twilight's last gleaming?

Whose broad stripes and bright stars thru the perilous fight,

O'er the ramparts we watched were so gallantly streaming?

And the rocket's red glare, the bombs bursting in air,

Gave proof through the night that our flag was still there.

Oh, say does that star-spangled banner yet wave

O'er the land of the free and the home of the brave.

FRANCIS SCOTT KEY
- 1814 -

Prologue

"THE HOME OF THE BRAVE"

It was not an occasion to inspire optimism. That evening, September 13, 1814, a young American lawyer and his two companions were standing on the deck of an American sloop in the midst of a British fleet in Baltimore harbor. Francis Scott Key and Colonel John S. Skinner had sailed to the fleet and had successfully negotiated the release of an American doctor being held as a prisoner of war. And now the three men were forbidden to return to shore. Pelted by wind and rain and the man-made lightning and thunder of warfare, the three Americans watched as sixteen Royal Navy frigates continued their daylong bombardment of Fort McHenry. This was a tense moment for these men personally, as well as for the young United States of America.

In its first three decades as a nation, the fledgling American republic was given some needed breathing room in foreign affairs to grow and solidify as a democracy. Following the loss of their American colonies, the British were diverted with other more pressing concerns closer to home, grappling with the effects of what was becoming a bloody revolution in France, their closest neighbor and historic adversary. The violence and anarchy of the French Revolution grew and eventually erupted into armed hostilities between France and most of its neighboring countries, including Great Britain.

Napoleon Bonaparte gained prominence as a talented general in these conflicts and emerged in 1799 as the de facto leader of France. After Napoleon crowned himself as the French emperor and assumed dictatorial powers in 1803, Britain joined a coalition of royalist European states in opposing Napoleon's military ambitions to extend French rule throughout Europe. For the next several years, battles raged back and forth across the continent and on the high seas.

America was pulled into the European conflict when Britain imposed blockades against maritime trade with France, stopping and impounding neutral ships, including American vessels. The growing harassment of American ships and disputes over other maritime issues brought the United States Congress to declare war on Great Britain on June 18, 1812. The United States failed in an attempt to invade Canada, and although American ships engaged British vessels in a few naval skirmishes along the Atlantic coast and on the Great Lakes, Britain remained focused on Europe and the ongoing war with Napoleonic France.

In 1814, England and its European allies defeated Napoleon and banished him to the Mediterranean island of Elba. The British then turned the full force of their military might on the war with America, initiating a series of attacks on the new nation's major east coast cities. In the late summer of 1814, British troops sacked Washington, burned the capitol and the President's mansion, and forced President James Madison and his wife Dolly to flee before the city was captured. The fires in Washington could be seen forty miles away in Baltimore, America's third largest city at the time and the next objective of the British forces. The British planned an assault that combined land troops moving toward Baltimore from Washington with the support and firepower of a large fleet lying offshore in Chesapeake Bay. Fort McHenry, guarding the entrance to Baltimore harbor and the first bastion of American defenses, was the first obstacle the British would face, and the walled fort would bear the brunt of the attack from the sea.

Before leaving Washington, the British arrested a Maryland doctor, Dr. William Beanes, claiming that he had been responsible for the American capture of British soldiers during the assault on Washington. Acting under the direction of American military leaders, Colonel John S. Skinner asked Francis Scott Key, a lawyer and friend of Dr. Beanes, to assist him in gaining the release of the imprisoned physician. After gathering letters written by wounded British prisoners of war describing the good treatment they had received at the hands of Dr. Beanes, Skinner and Key went to Baltimore. On September 4, they left on a sloop flying a flag of truce in search of the British fleet, which lay at anchor farther down Chesapeake Bay. Four days later, they found and boarded the British flagship, and after producing the pouch of letters, were successful in securing the doctor's release.

Even though the Americans had succeeded in rescuing Dr. Beanes, the British officers realized that Key, Skinner, and Dr. Beanes knew the location and size of their fleet; they feared the Americans may have overheard discussions about British plans. The British leaders decided to officially detain the Americans on board the flagship, and the fleet continued on to Baltimore with the American sloop in tow. Before the battle began, the three American men were allowed to re-board their own ship but were forbidden to return to shore. From this unusual perspective, Key and his comrades watched the attack on Fort McHenry.

British bombardment began at dawn on September 13 and lasted for twenty-five hours. The ships fired more than 1,500 bombshells with lighted fuses, exploding on or over the fort. The attack against the fort was unrelenting, but by sunset the Americans were still holding on and were starting to give back in kind. After several hours, American fire from the fort's cannons had sunk or damaged enough British vessels that the tide started to turn. The British began to have doubts about whether it was possible to continue the advance on Baltimore, and a standoff ensued. For a time, the cannonading stopped, but around one a.m. on the fourteenth, the British fleet roared back to life, "lighting the rainy night sky with grotesque fireworks."[1]

Watching with apprehension from their sloop, the three Americans knew that as long as the bombardment continued, Fort McHenry had not surrendered. Then, several hours before dawn, a sudden and mysterious silence fell over the scene. The American detainees did not know that the British officers had determined that Baltimore was becoming too costly a prize and had passed an order to the ships to cease firing and make plans for a retreat.

Because of the heavy rain, Major George Armistead, commander of Fort McHenry, had earlier flown a small "storm flag" from the mast of the fort. As the storm abated and the shelling ceased, Major Armistead ordered that an oversize flag he had previously commissioned from a Baltimore "maker of colors" be raised on the pole in an act of defiance.

Thus it was at "the dawn's early light" that an anxious Francis Scott Key peered through the clearing clouds and smoke and saw the waving "star-spangled banner" flying proudly over the fort. He knew that the "home of the brave" had conquered another challenge to its survival and future. It would not be the first nor the last time that the nation would pass through times that would "try men's souls."

NOTE

1. "Francis Scott Key," http://www.usflag.org/history/francisscottkey.html.

Preface

WE HAVE PASSED THIS WAY BEFORE

In late September 2008, residents of the United States suddenly faced an economic meltdown that many economists compared with the 1929 Wall Street crash that had led to the decade-long Great Depression. The dominos were beginning to fall. Slumping home values had exposed large and hidden weaknesses in the home mortgage industry. An accumulating number of "subprime" mortgages with now-worthless equity value threatened to bankrupt homeowners, the financial institutions that had given them mortgages, and the investors who had purchased those mortgages. Failing investment banks and related institutions that had over-leveraged the shaky assets represented by these mortgages arranged hasty mergers with stronger companies. Others faced bankruptcy if the government did not immediately intervene. Because many of the worthless mortgages had been bundled as investment instruments and bought by investors and funds in the United States and abroad, the entire world financial community was suffering a bad case of the jitters.

In the midst of the final weeks of the 2008 presidential campaign, accusations of blame flew in every direction, and Congress stayed in session for an unprecedented extra two weeks to hammer out legislation that would amount to a more than 700-billion-dollar federal government bailout for the financial industry. In spite of the legislation, stock markets around the world panicked and took a nosedive, and ordinary citizens throughout America looked at the shrinking values of their 401k plans and other investment accounts and feared for their own economic futures. The presidential candidates, Senators John McCain and Barack Obama, not being privy to all of the intricate moves and maneuvers underway in government and financial circles, did not (and probably could not) come up with much in the way of specific solutions, and in many ways seemed to be as helpless in these initial stages of the crisis as the average citizen. In the end, voters looked at the candidates' competing economic views and abilities, and a few weeks later chose Barack Obama to lead the nation out of the mess that his predecessors in Washington had helped create. As of this writing, the economy is, in the best-case scenarios, just beginning to inch away from the abyss, but difficult times appear to be in store for Americans.

As the economic downturn of 2008 and 2009 advanced into what looked like the beginning of a global depression, I found myself fascinated by our collective and individual responses to today's troubling and uncertain times. Many see clouds gathering on the horizon and express surprise—even shock—that the endless blue bowl of sunlit days may be coming to an unwelcome end. Anyone who was born after the 1930s has not seen such times or passed this way before. And, in confronting this and other "new" experiences, some rise up in righteous indignation and with the bravado of youth say, "bring 'em on." Others cower and withdraw in a painful paralysis born of fear and foreboding. In between these extremes are those who grasp the reality of the situation but still maintain a belief that we can find a way through the crises we face.

A great and important distinction exists between bravery and bravado—the first being real and deep, the second a cheap facsimile of the first. Bravado and paralyzing fear abound, and both, though opposite in nature, are the same gate to darker days. In Dante's *Divine Comedy*, the Roman poet Virgil gestured to Dante at the entrance to Hell to look up and read the inscription upon the gates: "Abandon Hope, All Ye Who Enter." Americans must have felt at times that they were literally standing at the gates of a Dantean inferno, and the economic crisis that began in 2008 may well look that way to many. But each time such challenges have arisen in the past, leaders and citizens have emerged who moved forward with faith and courage, confident of their ability to endure and eventually overcome.

Today clouds continue to gather, extending beyond the financial crisis and the uncertainty it has brought. Each day's news brings threatening weather that adds to that already darkening the skies—clouds portending of terrorism and increasing disregard for human life, polarization and tribalism, intolerance, greed and avarice, growing contempt for traditional patterns of human decency and respect, and many other fears. Most of us instinctively feel a desire to respond to the challenges, and the adrenaline starts pumping. Some, however, are concerned about our ability to successfully face and overcome the challenges that are producing these fears.

Before you find yourself responding to crisis times and events with fear and knee-jerk reactions, thoughtfully consider this book's premise. We are not the first people in Earth's history to encounter such situations, nor are we the first Americans to face major threats. This nation has passed this way before—many, many times before. As a nation, we have confronted and conquered the challenges of many such dark nights in our history, and the roots of those conquests have sprung from the lives of men and women in many ways very much like you and I and like whom we may become.

This is a book not about being brave, but about learning to be brave. It is about drawing from, rather than drawing down. It is about purposefulness in the face of seeming powerlessness. It is about a history, a legacy, and an opportunity. If we as Americans are willing to learn from those who have sailed through these storms before, we can, I believe, succeed. If not, we may find ourselves—both as a nation and as individuals—alone, unprotected, and unprepared for the storms that come into our lives.

Albert Einstein taught a key principle about facing adversity when he was once asked who he felt was the greater scientist and thinker, himself or Sir Isaac Newton. After some reflection, Einstein responded by paraphrasing Newton, "The dwarf sees farther than the giant when he stands on the shoulders of the giant." We too will see farther when we stand on the shoulders of those giants who have brought us to this point.

The United States of America is a nation of people who stand on the shoulders of many giants. If we are humble enough and thoughtful enough to be taught, these giants whisper a message for every generation—they whisper of hope and hard work, of understanding and living by correct principles, of conforming our lives to our better nature and to those eternal laws of nature and behavior that govern our world.

THE PARABLE OF THE LONE SAPLING

When I was a young man, at least once or twice a week, my route would take me along a large, open field of grain, and out in the completely exposed center of this expanse stood two trees. The one on the windward side, fully exposed to the dominant direction of the wind and the weather, was a large and well-worn oak. Its trunk was broad, its branches large and plentiful. In summer it was fully leafed in all the verdant glory that is an oak tree. On closer examination, I could see the scars of age and weather in its trunk and some of its damaged and dying branches. But, in general, it stood strong and solid, deeply rooted and well-suited to whatever weather Mother Nature would offer up.

Very close to the trunk of this gentle giant, nestled between its strong roots, a tiny sapling grew. Growing on the leeward side of the mighty oak had protected it from the winds and the weather. It was all alone. I am no arborist, but I do know that oak trees drop more than one acorn a season. Some, of course, are carried off by the wind, others are borne in the jaws or bellies of animals rooting in the tree's shadow. But of all the acorns that had fallen near the great oak over the years, this one alone had survived.

I cannot know for sure, but I can reasonably surmise why the lone sapling had survived. By nestling in the rich soil that gathered and stayed beneath the large oak's mighty roots, by standing on the leeward side—out of the punishing weather—and by staying close to the protection of the mighty trunk, this one little seedling lived, and, as I watched it over the years, it thrived and grew through year after year of rain, snow, sleet, harsh wind, and blistering sun. It grew strong because it stayed close to the old oak.

George Washington, Thomas Jefferson, John and Abigail Adams, Abraham Lincoln, Dr. Martin Luther King Jr., John F. Kennedy, Harry S. Truman, Ronald Reagan, and so many others, have been some of our mighty oaks—strongly rooted, with powerful trunks and long, full branches.

This book will draw from the examples of these and other leaders and explore the lessons they can teach us about facing challenging situations and major crises in our time—both as a nation and as individuals.

The land of the brave will continue to prosper if those who live in it are prepared to be courageous and decisive, and also if it is the land of the humble. Why humble? The questions we pose to you in this book reflect the need for both of these aspects: Are you willing and humble enough to learn from those who have gone before? Rather than rejecting and rebelling and reinventing the wheel—as so many seem to feel is both the right and the obligation of a rising generation—are you willing to recognize that there is much to be learned from those who confronted daunting challenges in the past? And in confronting challenges you face, can you apply the lessons and wisdom of those who have traveled this path before and made us a great nation?

The little sapling became a great tree on its own merits, in part by growing, developing, and stretching itself, but also by growing within the nurturing and sheltering environment of the great oak.

These pages represent an attempt to show what we can learn from some great oaks of the American experience and the challenges they weathered. My hope is that all of us might aspire to become the newest generation of the home of the brave.

PREFACE: Key Principles to Remember

Our history has taught us . . .

- America and Americans have confronted and conquered the challenges of many dark nights in our history.
- The conquest of these challenges has come from men and women who were very much like you—and the person whom you may become.
- When challenges come, you will see farther when you stand on the shoulders of those who have brought us to this point and learn from their experience. In the words of George Santayana, "Those who cannot learn from history are doomed to repeat it."
- Safety and success in challenging times come from standing with each other, as well as with the "mighty oaks" of the past—those leaders who withstood and survived the challenges of their day.

Chapter I

THE LEGACY

THE PILGRIMS—A VOYAGE INTO THE GREAT UNKNOWN

On Saturday, November 11, 1620, a lone sailing ship—the *Mayflower*—arrived at what is now called Provincetown Harbor, on the tip of Cape Cod, Massachusetts. On board the tiny ship were 102 souls—men, women, and children—their earthly belongings (including two dogs), and nearly exhausted provisions. After a long and difficult crossing, their arrival in this sheltered harbor heralded a respite from the very real storms of the North Atlantic.

This group of exiled Separatists had left the Church of England and moved to Holland, a more tolerant environment in which to practice their religion. Ultimately they decided to settle in the New World and then developed and put in motion plans to accomplish the voyage.

Before making landfall at Cape Cod, they had already faced some daunting challenges. Originally two ships had been contracted for the journey, the *Mayflower* and the *Speedwell.* After departing from Southampton in early August, problems with leaks on the *Speedwell* quickly forced them to put in at another English port for repairs. Resuming their journey in late August, they continued on until the *Speedwell* developed additional leaks more than two hundred miles west of Land's

End, the southwest tip of England. The two ships turned around and returned to Plymouth, the closest major port.

As time passed and autumn approached, the group decided to crowd everyone onto the *Mayflower* and cross the Atlantic alone. Even though they were leaving England late in the season, they were buoyed by the hope of establishing a colony in the New World where they could worship God, freed from the restraints they had encountered in England and Holland.

Crossing the storm-prone North Atlantic in a small craft can be a gut-wrenching experience, even in our day. Aboard a tiny, crowded ship little more than one hundred feet long and twenty-five feet wide, the 102 pilgrims endured two months of storm-tossed seas, increasingly cold weather, seasickness, and other ailments before they saw land on November 9.

The Pilgrims had planned to settle near the mouth of the Hudson River in what was then considered northern Virginia, but they actually made landfall more than two hundred miles northeast of that intended destination. Now it was mid-November. The weather had turned cold, and winter's full force would soon be upon them. They had neither time nor provisions to continue their voyage to the Hudson. To add to these considerations, their shallop, a small open boat needed for transport in shallow waters, needed repairs.

The events of the next few days and weeks would be critical for the survival of this little group of Pilgrims who had at last arrived in the New World. Their location at the tip of Cape Cod was not suitable for permanent settlement, being exposed to the fury of Atlantic storms, with limited land on a narrow peninsula comprised largely of sand.

Before leaving England, the Pilgrim leaders had discussed a contract with Captain John Smith, who had been one of the founders of Jamestown, Virginia, in 1607. Although Smith had mapped the coast of what is now New England and was better acquainted with the area than most men at that time, his seeming know-it-all and arrogant attitude put off the Pilgrims. In the words of historian Nathaniel Philbrick, "Smith possessed a strong personality, and [the Pilgrim leaders feared] a man of his worldly nature might come to dominate what they intended to be an inherently religious enclave."[1]

Smith lost the contract to Miles Standish, who was less expensive and, upon initial impressions, was more of a style and sensibility the Pilgrims preferred. But after arriving in the New World, they soon realized that Standish did not possess any practical knowledge of where they were and where they needed to go.

Their somewhat precarious situation did not daunt the little band. They first endeavored to find a more suitable location for settlement. Temporarily unable to use their shallow-water boat, land-based exploring parties followed the curving hook of the cape. While journeying south along Cape Cod they discovered evidence of earlier Europeans, native graves, and, in "an area where the sand had recently been patted smooth," they found a cache of dried seed corn buried there by the Indians. They filled a large cast iron pot with corn, as preparation against what they sensed would be an early and aggressive winter. While modern readers might question the notion of people taking for their own use provisions laid up for winter by someone else, Philbrick notes the precarious situation in which the Pilgrims found themselves:

> Many, if not most European settlers in a similar situation would have had enough faith in their own, supposedly superior, technology that they would have had no use for a buried bag of Native seed. But the Pilgrims were not usual European immigrants. For one thing, they were desperate. Due to the woeful state of their provisions, as well as the lateness of the season, they knew they were in a survival situation from the start. . . . They were willing to try just about anything if it meant they might survive their first year.[2]

That pragmatic attitude and an abiding faith that they could succeed turned out to be the Pilgrims' salvation. By November 27, the repairs to the shallop were complete, and a second exploration party set off by sea along the coast of Cape Cod Bay, holding tight to the shallows. In addition to looking for a settlement site, they returned to the corn cache and retrieved an additional supply, augmented by a second cache they discovered nearby.

But in just sixteen days, the weather had begun to change dramatically. One morning, the exploring party awoke to six inches of snow on the ground. Winter was coming on swiftly. This second attempt to locate a settlement site was aborted, and the exploratory group returned to the relative warmth of the *Mayflower*.

It took the Pilgrims well into December to find a suitable location, move their ship and people to the new site, and establish their initial settlement at Plymouth. Every day since their arrival at Provincetown Harbor, life had become harsher and more difficult, and the situation looming before them now was one of increasing challenge. Because of the lateness of the season and scarcity of provisions, returning to England was not an option for the Pilgrims. All they were able to do was erect what shelter they could and somehow make it through the winter.

Once winter set in, disease and death arrived in full fury. Many became ill, and many of those died. At one point, according to Philbrick, "so many fell ill that there were barely half a dozen left to tend the sick. Progress on the houses fell to a standstill as the healthy ones became full-time nurses—preparing meals, tending fires, washing the 'loathsome clothes,' and emptying chamber pots."[3]

Despite the weather and appalling conditions, these great women and men, acting as fathers, mothers, sisters, brothers, and nursemaids to each other, dug in and bent themselves to their great task with a bravery and an attitude best described by William Bradford, governor of the tiny Plymouth colony:

> And yet the Lord so upheld these persons as in this general calamity they were not all infected either with sickness or lameness. And

> what I have said of these I may say of many others who died in this general visitation, and others yet living, that whilst they had health, yea or any strength continuing, they were not wanting to any that had need of them. And I doubt not that their recompense is with the Lord.[4]

The story of the courage, faith, and determination of the Pilgrims represents the birth of the legacy that has been bequeathed to us—the first of our founding mothers and fathers and representative of all of their cultural offspring who followed. Beset by weather and cold and mounting starvation, and ravaged by disease, they bravely battled on, in Bradford's words, "whilst they had health . . . or *any* strength continuing."[5] And they not only battled for personal survival, but also, "they were not wanting to any that had need of them."

As you confront your own challenges today or in a future day you do not yet know, you need to understand who we as Americans are. We are the progeny of these and others who came in those early years. Like them, we have individual weaknesses, foibles, and personal problems, but also, like them, we can rise above our challenges, if we will.

The terrible pain of that first winter, after a stormy crossing and the difficulties in locating and establishing a settlement, is almost impossible for me to comprehend. I have been sick, but I have confronted my sickness in the arms of modern medicine, in a home or medical facility with heat and clean water and strong shelter from the elements. And I have felt challenged enough to complain, but those complaints shamed and changed me when I read of our Pilgrim forebears—of their legacy of bravery in the face of environmental challenges and unspeakable suffering. And I am filled with the hope that I can learn and try to develop my own fledgling bravery in the face of difficulties we all may have to face.

The Pilgrim settlers of New England, along with the earlier commercial settlement at Jamestown by the Virginia Company, represented the beginning of the British colonization of North America. The Pilgrims were soon joined on Massachusetts Bay by a large influx of Puritans, a diverse group of English citizens who had their own issues with the Anglican church over purity of doctrine and religious agency. They too sought a place where they could worship as they chose. Starting in 1630, ten years after the Pilgrims, Puritans in large numbers settled Boston and established many communities north of the Plymouth Plantation, as it had come to be known. The entire area became part of what was called the Massachusetts Bay Colony, and Puritan colonists expanded their settlement into much of what is now Massachusetts, Rhode Island, and Connecticut.

In the century that followed, a flood of groups and individual immigrants from Britain and Holland established colonies along the Atlantic coast, some formed by religious groups, others motivated by commercial, mercantile, or maritime possibilities. By 1750, these colonies were home to an estimated 1.2 million people, forming the nucleus of a unique culture and society that stretched from New England to Georgia.

By the early 1770s, a century and a half after the Pilgrims and other early settlers courageously established a foothold for what would become the United States of America, some of their equally courageous and remarkable descendents came together to forge a new nation and establish a firm foundation for the freedoms that America has come to represent. Their struggles were not against the elements or native inhabitants, but rather for the hearts and minds of the colonists, persuading them of the need to become an independent nation. Before their efforts were ultimately successful, the cause of independence they espoused became a struggle involving blood and sacrifice.

For the citizens of these thirteen British colonies in America, the time was ripe for major change. Ready and able to govern themselves, many colonists resented being ruled by legislative fiat from London.

Without colonial representation, Parliament imposed taxes that fanned resentment among the colonists. The British also forced the Americans to fund and house British troops, supposedly there for the purpose of providing protection, but actually there to keep the colonists under control.

Neither Parliament nor the king paid much heed to American wishes or interests. It was time to identify and establish a new and better way of governing a people. Throughout the 1770s, brave men and women, their efforts fraught with risk and uncertainty, would free the colonies from British rule and establish a government "of the people, by the people, and for the people." What they accomplished became a light to similarly oppressed people in Europe, South America, and elsewhere. Revolution would eventually move western civilization beyond the initiative-stifling tyrannies and injustices of centuries of rule by despotic kings or a privileged few.

ABIGAIL ADAMS—A PATRIOT PARTNER AND EARLY FIGHTER FOR RIGHT

Because much of history focuses on "his" story, we tend to forget the women who also strove to bring freedom to colonial America. The roles these women played created part of the legacy we examine in this small book. These women represent many of the mighty oaks in whose shadow our country thrives. And one of the great oak trees of colonial times was certainly Abigail Adams.

Her husband John, one of our founding fathers and second president of this country, has been much in the media of late—the result of a powerfully written and wonderfully performed HBO miniseries based on the masterful biography *John Adams* by David McCullough.

We hear and know much of John Adams's contributions, but with a little bit of study, we learn the integral part Abigail Adams played in exerting her own bravery to both mold and encourage her husband

and to confront the challenges of her own life and the times in which she lived.

The following excerpt from a letter penned by the young John Adams a month before their wedding demonstrates Abigail Adams's import and her person. They had been apart for a number of weeks:

> Oh, my dear girl, I thank heaven that another fortnight will restore you to me—after so long a separation. My soul and body have both been thrown into disorder by your absence, and a month or two more would make me the most insufferable cynic in the world. I see nothing but faults, follies, frailties and defects in anybody lately. People have lost all their good properties or I my justice or discernment.[6]

This reflects an extremely accurate personal insight into the troubles of personality that afflicted Mr. Adams most of his life, troubles that Abigail tempered well, as evidenced by the next paragraph:

> But you who have always softened and warmed my heart, shall restore my benevolence as well as my health and tranquility of mind. You shall polish and refine my sentiments of life and manners, banish all the unsocial and ill natured particles in my composition, and form me to that happy temper that can reconcile a quick discernment, with perfect candor.[7]

In the context of this letter and their lifelong marriage, McCullough writes,

> His marriage to Abigail Smith was the most important decision of John Adams's life, as would become apparent with time. She was in all respects his equal and the part she was to play would be greater than he could possibly have imagined, for all his love for her and what appreciation he already had of her beneficial, steadying influence.[8]

Abigail also played a role in a long-term challenge in American history that might qualify as the darkest and most dangerous of all—the horrible legacy of slavery. The nation waged its only civil war in part over this legacy. It still casts its shadow over us today, although in the last half century we have made progress in overcoming it. An additional glimmer of light seems to be breaking with the election of a black President and the dawning of new generations of Americans more open than ever to Thomas Jefferson's declaration of the truth that "all men are created equal, that they are endowed by their Creator with certain unalienable Rights."

The American struggle against this darkness has many forebears, including early abolitionists, Abraham Lincoln, Dr. Martin Luther King Jr., and other modern-day civil rights crusaders. But this battle began nearly two centuries before Selma with the bravery of Abigail Adams. In her struggle against slavery, she would not only confront and conquer this great evil in a small and personal way, but without knowing it, she was setting an example and preparing the way for her son John Quincy Adams, our fourth president and an early opponent of slavery, to pass a torch that would eventually pass to Abraham Lincoln and later to Dr. King and others still bravely engaged in this critical challenge.

Once again, from McCullough:

> In a particularly memorable letter, she recounted a crisis that arose when the youngest of her hired hands, James Prince, a free black boy she had taken under her wing in Philadelphia, came to ask if he might attend evening class in town at a new school for apprentices. Abigail, who had taught him herself to read and write, warmly approved, but was soon asked by a neighbor to withdraw James. If she did not, she was told, the other boys would refuse to attend and the school would close. Had James misbehaved, Abigail asked. No, she was informed, it was because he was black. Did these other boys object when he attended church? No, they did not.
>
> "The boy is a freeman as much as any of the young men, and merely because his face is black is he to be denied instruction?" she asked. "How is he to be qualified to procure a livelihood? Is this the Christian principle of doing unto others as we would have others to do to us?"

> She requested that all the boys be sent to her. "Tell them . . . that I hope we shall all go to Heaven together." And this, she was pleased to report to Adams, ended the crisis. She heard no more on the subject; James continued in the school.[9]

Born of one of the great and noble families of the early Massachusetts Bay colony but familiar both in theory and experience with the hardscrabble life of colonial existence, this intelligent and brave woman was the living embodiment of the iron hand in the velvet glove. She was unafraid to confront and conquer injustice, regardless of personal cost or consequence.

GEORGE WASHINGTON—STEADFAST AGAINST GREAT ODDS

We live in an age where one of the prevalent ways of dealing with difficult and challenging times is to retreat from them—to retire and, if fortune favors, to do so as quickly as possible. Some in our time have brought together prosperity and the lure of the Sunbelt in a widely held belief that the later years of life should be about withdrawal and retreat into leisure living. But there are times and events that require us to be engaged in the affairs of our country throughout our lives, as exemplified by the life of America's first President.

George Washington was a lifelong admirer of the ancient Roman consul, Lucius Quinctius Cincinnatus. One of Washington's great desires was to emulate this gentleman farmer and military leader of ancient Rome by serving with honor and then, like his hero, withdrawing from public life to live out the balance of his years on his farm—in modern parlance, to retire. Washington didn't lack for attempts to achieve this objective, but he struggled considerably in actually securing the prize.

In the early days of the Continental Congress, John Adams pushed his fellow patriots to seek redress for the British horrors in the battles of Bunker Hill, Lexington, and Concord, and to form a Continental Army. Washington, the gentleman farmer, stood up and pledged his dedicated service in forming such an army, fighting and winning the battles to come—all at great personal cost. Although known as a man of integrity and honor, Washington was not one to seek the limelight. But he had served as an officer during the French and Indian War of the 1750s, and like Cincinnatus, his personal character required him to step forward when his countrymen called.

Interestingly, events would show that George Washington was not a great field commander, but he had other essential leadership qualities. As historian Paul Johnson put it, "He fought in all nine general actions, and lost all but three of them. But he was a strategist. He realized that his supreme task was to train an army, keep it in the field, supply it, and pay it."[10]

Washington faced the additional challenge of recruiting volunteer troops and keeping them from leaving the fray when their enlistments were up. The war would drag on more than eight years, with the Americans and British locked in an endurance contest. Keeping the Continental Army at adequate strength and suitably equipped was an ongoing challenge for Washington.

The Continental Army fought seesaw battles in upstate New York, New Jersey, Pennsylvania, and the southern states. After France's intervention on behalf of the Americans, British resolve gradually dwindled to the point where public opinion in England and pressures from enemies abroad induced the British to withdraw from the fight. When Lord Cornwallis surrendered to Washington at Yorktown, Virginia, on October 19, 1781, the fighting on American soil came to a halt.

Even in the worst of times, Washington did not flinch. After tasting success in forcing the British out of Boston in March of 1776, the army of the thirteen newly declared "United States of America" suffered defeat after defeat, losing New York and much of New Jersey before the end of the year, being driven almost to Philadelphia before winter weather closed in. With British troops and their German mercenaries settled and off guard in Princeton and Trenton, New Jersey, it would have been easy to move into winter quarters and sit out the snow and cold. Instead, Washington mounted a daring raid across the ice-choked Delaware River the day after Christmas and routed or captured the British and German troops. This singular victory turned the tide for the Americans at the end of a particularly discouraging year. Within a month, the Continental Army had recaptured most of New Jersey.

In 1777 the tide turned again, and Philadelphia ended up in British hands. The winter of 1777–78 found the Continental Army encamped at Valley Forge, Pennsylvania—perhaps the lowest of Washington's many low points in the conflict. Here, as in the rest of the war, he continued to be a tireless and inspiring leader, choosing to live in a tent in below-freezing temperatures until all of his troops had log huts to sleep in. Through this and other decisions and actions, Washington exhibited the kind of caring that won the loyalty of what was starting to become a formidable fighting force.

His soldiers, in turn, responded to his leadership. In a later battle in the war, Washington was bringing reinforcements to the front and encountered a corps of soldiers retreating. He called a halt and rode his horse up and down the line, exhorting the troops until his mount dropped from exhaustion. He seemed to be everywhere at once. As the Marquis de Lafayette described, "[Washington rode] all along the lines amid the shouts of the soldiers, cheering them by his voice and restoring . . . the fortunes of the fight. I thought then, as now, that never had I beheld so superb a man."[11]

Paul Johnson notes an added dimension to Washington's leadership: "In addition, he gave the war, on the American side, a dignity which even his opponents recognized. He did nothing common, or mean, or cruel, or vengeful. He behaved, from first to last, like a gentleman."[12]

Following the British surrender, and after eight years of war and all George Washington had endured and done, he desired again to retire to the comfort and pastoral pleasures of his beloved Mt. Vernon, yet he still did not shirk calls to duty. When asked to serve his country in his later years, he responded, presiding over the Constitutional Convention in 1785 and serving two terms as the first President of the United States of America.

Always a modest man, he refused popular acclaim to be installed as an almost literal king. After his election, George Washington took the oath of office as President and set a remarkable precedent for future Presidents to follow. Near the end of his first term, he prepared his letter of resignation, but when asked to serve again, he bravely and privately filed it away.

Finally, in 1796, nearing the end of his second term, he published the resignation letter, forcing the hand of the Congress to allow him a retreat to his home and farm overlooking the Potomac River. Unfortunately, while riding the boundaries of his property at Mt. Vernon three years later, rain soaked him through. Failing to remove his rain-drenched clothing, he caught a severe cold. Early in the evening of December 14, 1799, this brave "Father of his country" finally retired to his ultimate reward and, in lieu of his farm and fields at Mt. Vernon, the Elysian fields so beloved by his Roman spiritual forebear.

Like the great oak tree, weathering season after season of storms, we are rooted in a legacy founded in the likes of our Pilgrim forebears, of women like Abigail Adams and of men like General Washington. These and many others who lived in colonial and revolutionary America bear the trademark of those we honor and seek to emulate: the bravery to confront and conquer difficult circumstances—not for just a moment and not without struggle and personal sacrifice, but with courage to continue honorably until triumphant.

This legacy is the foundation of the American national premise. We must reach deep into our individual selves and find and nurture the tiniest seeds of bravery. If we do not yet believe we are capable of lives such as these, we must begin to believe—or at least have the desire to believe—who we may *become* if we will but bend ourselves to the challenge.

THE LEGACY: Key Principles to Remember

The Pilgrims taught us . . .

STICK TOGETHER

- The traditional responses to a threat are "flight" or "fight." Either of these responses will tear us apart and can harm us individually and collectively.
- The Pilgrims, in the face of a brutal winter where they would nearly starve and freeze, chose to come together as a united team. By sticking together, we can support each other.

Abigail Adams taught us . . .

DEFEND WHAT IS RIGHT

- She would not stand for the evil that was slavery and racism. Throughout her life, she fought to treat all men as "created equal and endowed by their Creator with certain unalienable rights." Her persistent example set a model for her son John Quincy Adams, who would rise to the defense of the slaves in years to come.

THE LEGACY: Key Principles to Remember

(continued)

General George Washington taught us . . .

SACRIFICE

- Difficult times can become exhausting times because of how much they demand in the way of physical, financial, emotional, mental, and spiritual strength. Exhausted by his extensive personal commitment to the Revolutionary War, the principles in the Declaration of Independence, and the wishes of the Continental Congress, Washington had earned retirement and respite at Mt. Vernon. Instead, he sacrificed his personal desires to accept one last call to serve America as its first President, to the blessing and benefit of the nation.

NOTES

1. Nathaniel Philbrick, *Mayflower: A Story of Courage, Community, and War* (New York: Viking, 2006), 59.
2. Ibid., 64.
3. Ibid., 85.
4. Ibid., 85–86.
5. Ibid., emphasis added.
6. David McCullough, *John Adams* (New York: Simon & Schuster, 2001), 57.
7. Ibid.
8. Ibid.
9. Ibid., 480.
10. Paul Johnson, *A History of the American People* (New York: HarperCollins, 1998), 159–60.
11. Bart McDowell, *The Revolutionary War* (Washington, DC: The National Geographic Society, 1967), 136.
12. Johnson, *History of the American People*, 160.

Chapter II

THE LENS

I have sung the words of "The Star-Spangled Banner" probably hundreds of times since I first learned them as a preschooler. Over the years, I have come to realize that my attachment to this anthem and the events and sights it portrays has to do with what its author *chose* to write about in the tumultuous events of September 13 and 14, 1814.

As you will recall from the prologue of this book, Francis Scott Key was at the time a prisoner on a ship in an enemy fleet, deprived for the moment of his own liberty, helpless in the midst of all the explosions and the terror of the attack on Fort McHenry. But instead of focusing on the chaos and uncertainty around him, Key chose to focus on the flag. Instead of looking through the lens of hopelessness, fear, and despair, he saw what was happening through the lens of hope. He saw beyond the grim situation at hand and realized that the battle had not been lost, victory was possible, and the young American nation would survive. I am amazed that he chose to see and remember not the chaos, but the flag and what it symbolized. This focus produced the motivation to record his feelings through the poem that has since come to be the words of America's national anthem.

We often find ourselves in the midst of life's battles, beset by exploding expectations and challenges on every side. Too often we view our situation through the lens of hopelessness or despair and lose sight of the possibilities and opportunities that remain—what is *not* in chaos, what is *not* under threat, what is *not* falling apart all around us. But all too often it seems that all we can see are the exploding bombs and the rockets, and we fail to see that our personal flag—the symbol of our own hope and courage—is still there.

THE GALILEO REALITY MODEL: LENSES FOR SEEING CLEARLY

For much of the past two decades, I have been involved in teaching others how to use a valuable life tool that can help people clearly see what is going on around them. With the guidance and help of other talented and skilled professionals, I have been part of building a consulting business, The Galileo Initiative, based on a concept and lens-viewing tool we call The Galileo Reality Model. We gave the model this name in honor of Galileo Galilei, the sixteenth-century astronomer and inventor of telescopes who helped people see the physical world and universe through a different and more accurate lens.

The Reality Model teaches us that, like Francis Scott Key, the direction our lives take—especially in the face of challenge—directly relates as much to how we see and respond to the challenge as to what the challenge itself may be.

The following graphic illustrates how the model works:

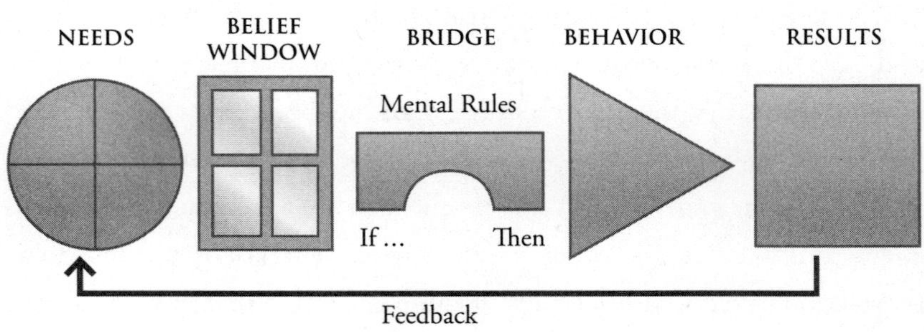

THE NEEDS WHEEL

All human behavior is driven by basic needs, represented on the model by the circular Needs Wheel. Whether our needs fall into a pyramid as Abraham Maslow proposed or whether they are listed as "live, love, learn and leave a legacy" like Dr. Stephen Covey suggested in *The 7 Habits of Highly Effective People*, the bottom-line reality is this: We all have needs. These needs drive all of our behavior; it is often done subconsciously, but everything we do every minute of every day is being pushed or driven by one or more of these basic needs.

For our purposes, we will label the fundamental needs as

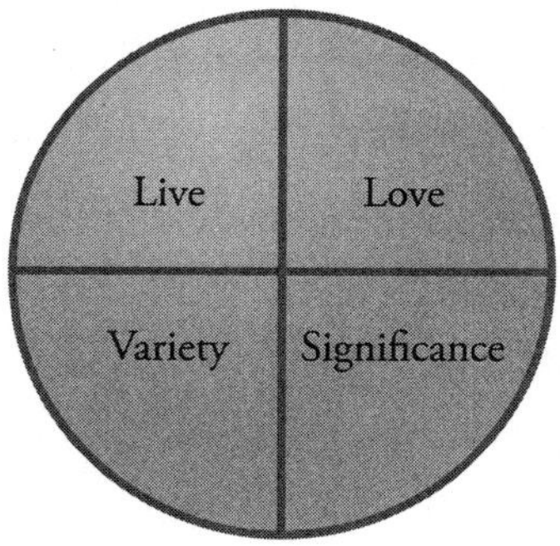

- The need to LIVE—including our need for safety, security, food, shelter, and so on. But, especially in a modern society, it includes the need for manageable mortgages and debt, job security, reasonable pay, and so on.
- The need to LOVE—deep, personal love as well as the love we share with friends, family, coworkers, and even pets.
- The need for VARIETY—causing us to own a TV remote, have more than one suit or pair of jeans, or travel to faraway places. Variety, as they say, is the spice of life. Although some need more spice than others, this need is very much a driver of human behavior.
- The need for SIGNIFICANCE—the desire to make a difference or have meaning in our lives. This need drives activities like the raising of children, community or military service, religious or spiritual inquiry, and many forms of personal

sacrifice and contribution. Covey calls this need "the need to leave a legacy."

THE BELIEF WINDOW AND BRIDGE:
HOW NEEDS ARE MET OR BETRAYED

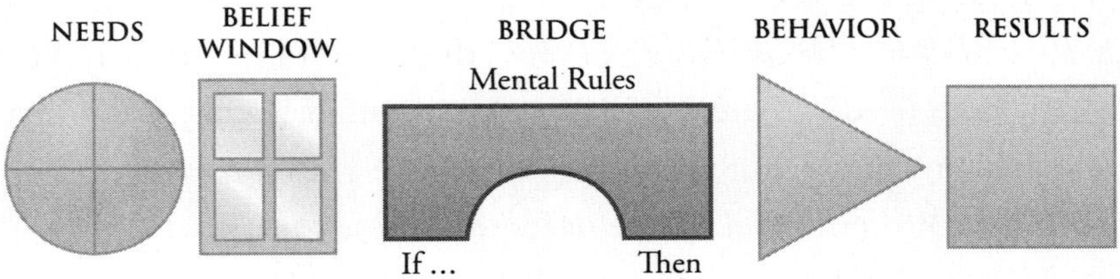

In the center of the Reality Model is a bridge. Notice above the bridge the phrase "mental rules" and below the bridge the words "If . . . Then." The bridge is a mechanism for connecting the front end of the model, needs and beliefs—which we will discuss in a moment—with behaviors and results. Our mind is interested, as is our whole being, with continued existence, and so over time it has learned that an if/then mechanism we call mental rules is key to that desired survival. Here's how the bridge works:

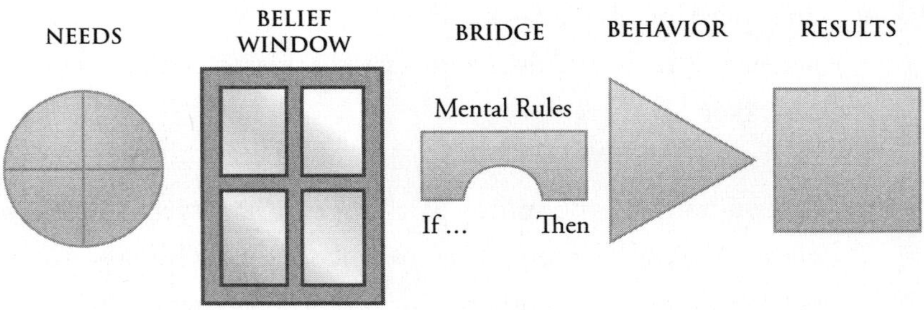

To the left of the bridge is something we call the Belief Window. The Belief Window is metaphorical, but we each have one. You can picture it as about two feet wide and three feet long, extending from a point just above your eyes to the middle of your chest, and permanently attached to your head, directly in front of your eyes. Wherever you look or turn, the window moves with you—you cannot look over, under, or around this window. You have had this invisible attachment since birth. Starting with early childhood, when you began to be aware of your world and started to try to figure it out, your perception of all of life's experiences have passed through that window. As you process these experiences, you gain insights about life and write them as "principles" on your Belief Window. By putting them on the window rather than in a mental pocket or corner of our brain, they are now readily available for review and application the next time a similar experience appears in front of the window.

Let me give you an example of this experience/awareness/principles process: Imagine you are walking down a public sidewalk, not paying much attention to what is going on around you. You look up, and there, about a half block ahead of you on the same sidewalk, is a large dog—a Doberman. No collar, no chain, no owner—just a Doberman casually ambling down the sidewalk toward you. Think about what you would do:

- Would you keep walking, with no change in your behavior?
- Would you feel the impulse to run, even if you didn't act on it?
- Would you prudently step into the nearest doorway or cross the street to avoid the dog?
- Would you run toward the Doberman, hand outstretched, cooing, "Oh, look! What a beautiful dog!"

What you would do is *triggered* by the dog but *determined* by the principles you have written on your window about Dobermans and dogs in general. This principle is the product of prior experience, and it doesn't have to be prior *direct* experience. Your sum total of experience with Dobermans could reside in what you have read, heard, or seen in movies or on TV. Secondary experience builds principles on your Belief Window as powerfully as primary experience.

Let's take two of the above responses and run them through the model, and you will see the function of the bridge at work.

Principle on my Belief Window: Dobermans *might* be dangerous.

Bridge: *If* Dobermans might be dangerous, *then* what will I do if I encounter one?

This brings us to another piece of the model: Behavior. Our behavior does not occur randomly, accidentally, or in a vacuum; it is the product of a principle on our Belief Window being exposed to the if/then process of our mental rules on the Reality Model's bridge:

Bridge: *If* Dobermans might be dangerous, *then* I will cross the street or step into a doorway, caution being the prudent course. The resulting behavior would be consistent with what is on my window.

Bridge: *If* I believe Dobermans *are* dangerous, *then* what will I do? I will run for my life.

Now, let's complete the model. If my behavior is to run, what will be the result? The Doberman will chase me. Why? Because he also has a Belief Window filled with principles inherited from his wolf ancestors, including the principle "Things that run are prey." Well, *if* things that run are prey, *then* the Doberman will chase me, and, unless I am very fit and extremely fast, he will catch me.

Remember, throughout your life, all of these collected needs and beliefs are driving your decisions and your actions. Whether you are consciously aware of them or not, they are at work.

So, at the far end of the model are Results—the measurable outcomes we experience each day. Results matter because results separate a good day from a bad one, a great relationship from an awkward one, a promising future from a foreboding one. We all want favorable results.

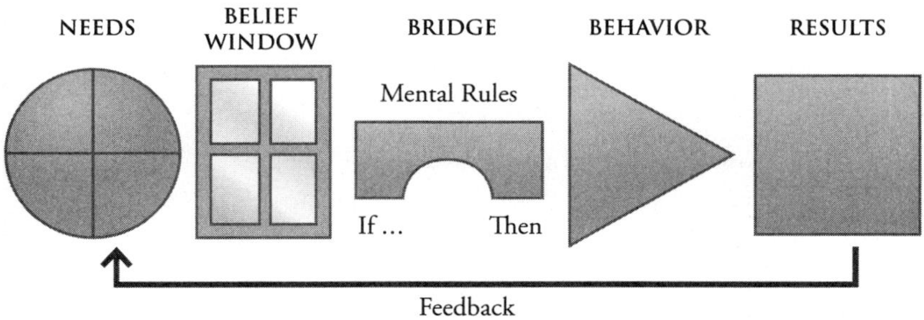

When it comes to results, the desired outcome is often simple to describe, although much harder to achieve. Note the feedback line running under the model connecting Needs at the front end and Results at the back. We are all trying (mostly unaware that we are doing so) to produce results that meet our needs. Think about the difference in both experience and feeling when results meet needs and when they don't. Think about the difference between an A on a paper and an F. For most of us, an A meets—and the F fails to meet—a basic need. (Depending on Dad's response to bad grades, it might be "the need to live"!)

THE CRITICAL QUESTION TO ASK OURSELVES

The Reality Model pushes us to ask a critical question. But to fully understand that question, let's talk first about needs and how we meet them. Keep in mind that all behavior, including that of the Doberman, produces a result. We have already said that we want to produce results that meet our needs (remember the feedback line). But the first thing we need to ask ourselves is whether or not the results of our behavior will meet our needs, not just now, but our needs *over time.*

The concept of "over time" brings out an interesting phenomenon of human experience. Too often, I believe, we focus on short-term results that work right now—even if they don't work later. Smokers tell me the initial nicotine hit from a freshly lit cigarette never gets old—it meets an immediate need with a pleasurable result—but does the looming and increasing threat of lung cancer or heart disease meet their needs *over time*? The action at the blackjack table has, for the players I have observed, an immediate and palpable thrill. Casinos include blackjack because the house knows the odds are in their favor. For many players, next month's mortgage payment or the kids' college funds are too often consumed in the excitement of the short term—and the results definitely do not meet their needs over time.

The mechanism of the Reality Model takes a little work to understand; the message does not. First of all, you should work to eliminate any principles on your Belief Window generating behaviors that produce short-term gain but end up producing long-term pain. Principles that drive long-term effectiveness, principles that build your life and drive maturity, are those that "meet your needs over time" and are truly a valuable acquisition in a challenging world.

Most of us have accumulated a lot of beliefs on our Belief Windows. And, as we have learned, many of those beliefs are invisible to us and to others; nevertheless, they are lenses through which we see life. They are driving our behavior and creating the results we are getting. As you read this book, keep in mind that you are reading it through your own Belief Window. What you take away from the experience is colored by everything you have written on that window since childhood—including your perceptions about the value (or lack thereof) of anything that comes from a book like this, or your inner beliefs about whether or not you have the power to make real changes in your life.

For practical purposes, you can divide your beliefs into two major categories:

- **Blocking Beliefs**, those foggy or distorted lenses that prevent you from confronting and conquering difficult situations in your life.

- **Unleashing Beliefs**, the clear lenses that literally unleash your abilities and allow you to behave in ways that create the results you seek.

Blocking beliefs restrict you to seeing only the bombs bursting in air and the rockets' red glare. Unleashing beliefs don't ignore the firefight, but they help you see the flag; they can give you hope where others may have given in to despair and dissolution.

One of the blessings and, I believe, challenges of living in a free country is the opportunity of believing as one wishes. How many times have you heard something like this: "It's a free country. I can believe anything I want to. You can't tell me what I should believe." All of which is true—if you don't care about clear lenses and results that lead to truly conquering your challenges. Because your beliefs drive behavior that creates your results, you can use your freedom to sustain your current manner of reacting and the results that approach is producing. Or, you can ask the defining question of the Galileo Reality Model:

Which of these beliefs will drive behavior that will best meet my needs over time?

My own experiences have shown me that finding the answer to that question is an individual process of discovery. I would like to share some of my personal answers to the question, but first let's consider two important overarching principles that govern how successfully you meet your needs over time.

1. CHOOSE REALITY, NOT JUST HOPE—THE LENS OF TRUTH

A respected religious leader who has been a mentor and strong influence in my life recently wrote a book called *Standing For Something.* The book, nationally published and written primarily to youth and young adults, reminds readers that declaring everything acceptable or valid may feel good, but it does not create the strength of character that produces the stability needed to confront a challenging world. It has become popular, in the name of openness, diversity, and inclusion, to declare all ways of thinking and believing to have equal value, but I have to disagree. Not all the things you choose to believe will meet your needs over time. Not every idea, including opposites, can be right—and I believe there is such a thing as right and wrong. I also believe there is such a thing as reality—which I define as

Things as they really are, not necessarily as we wish they were or want them to be.

John A. Widtsoe, a noted chemist and soil biologist in the first half of the twentieth century, explained the importance of seeing and understanding "things as they really are" in these insightful words, written in 1943 during the dark days of World War II:

> Civilization and enlightenment have come when men, using the experimental method, have begun to test the correctness of their beliefs. The highway to truth is paved with such rigid tests.
>
> On the contrary, the black cloud of superstition and confusion, twin enemies of progress, has obscured human vision when untested opinions or unverified claims or personal guesses have ruled human actions, or when assumed authority has claimed precedence over patient inquiry. The blind acceptance of unsupported statements, or placing theories on a pedestal for human worship, has always been a source of sorrow.
>
> Whenever men have set up devices or experiments to test the validity of their opinions, whenever men have demanded proofs of the verity of offered teachings, the world has moved forward. To test [then] current beliefs, Galileo dropped stones of unequal weights from a height; Lavoisier weighed mercury before and after heating; Pasteur filtered air through tufts of cotton; Lister washed wounds with a solution of carbolic acid—and each destroyed a false belief and revealed a new truth: stones of all sizes fall through the air with equal velocity; mercury becomes heavier when heated in air; microscopic living things, in the air, are often capable of injury to man; in wounds are germs which

> if not destroyed may delay healing. Out of each of these experiments a vast volume of truth has grown. . . .
>
> The same principle appears in the field of living things. . . . The complex relationships of social living must be tested for their value, if the path of safety is to be found. Though experimentation in this field is somewhat difficult because of the human will (the power to accept or reject) yet, for example, the desirability of organization, cooperation, and democracy, and the ill effects of autocracy, tyranny, and dictatorships, have been demonstrated by actual trial.[1]

2. CHOOSE RIGHT OVER WRONG—THE MORAL LENS

One of my heroes is the English scholar and author C.S. Lewis. His insights into life, philosophy, and the concept of right and wrong have profoundly affected me. Reading any of his books, papers, or talks immerses you in the depths of his genius. In his book *Mere Christianity,* he addresses the concept of right and wrong in the following exchange:

> Every one has heard people quarrelling. Sometimes it sounds funny and sometimes it sounds merely unpleasant; but however it sounds, I believe we can learn something very important from listening to the kinds of things they say. They say things like this: "How'd you like it if anyone did the same to you?"—"That's my seat, I was there first"—"Leave him alone, he isn't doing you any harm"—"Why should you shove in first?"—"Give me a bit of your orange, I gave you a bit of mine"—"Come on, you promised." People say things like that every day, educated people as well as uneducated, and children as well as grown-ups.
>
> Now what interests me about all these remarks is that the man who makes them is not merely saying that the other man's behaviour does not happen to please him. He is appealing to some kind of standard of behaviour which he expects the other man to know about. And the other man very seldom replies: "To hell with your standard." Nearly always he tries to make out that what he has been doing does not really go against the standard, or that if it does there is some special excuse. He pretends there is some special reason in this particular case why the

> person who took the seat first should not keep it, or that things were quite different when he was given the bit of orange, or that something has turned up which lets him off keeping his promise. It looks, in fact, very much as if both parties had in mind some kind of Law or Rule of fair play or decent behaviour or morality or whatever you like to call it, about which they really agreed. And they have. If they had not, they might, of course, fight like animals, but they could not quarrel in the human sense of the word. Quarrelling means trying to show that the other man is in the wrong. And there would be no sense in trying to do that unless you and he had some sort of agreement as to what Right and Wrong are; just as there would be no sense in saying that a footballer had committed a foul unless there was some agreement about the rules of football.[2]

Without a principle on your Belief Window addressing right and wrong and actions that reflect your choices, you are like a spinning top with a damaged spindle—unable to maintain balance and contact with a solid grounding. Like a top in this condition, you first wobble, then spin wildly out of control, and finally collapse. Think of how many times in the face of challenge, you or others you know have wobbled, spun wildly askew, and collapsed.

Challenging and difficult times can be exhausting but need not be overwhelming. If you can get the right principles and beliefs written on your window, you can weather the storm. But, who's to say what's "right"? Finding the principles that will best meet *your* needs over time is a matter of personal discovery. Here are some suggestions, as promised. Keep in mind that the following are examples from my own experiences and observations. You will need to find and clarify and write your own set of principles and beliefs—clear lenses that can guide you through your challenging times.

START EARLY TO FIND UNLEASHING BELIEFS

A source of unleashing beliefs for me are the writers and thinkers who guided our nation's Founding Fathers. When a gentleman farmer from Virginia spread parchment across his lap desk in the summer of 1776 and penned the words, "We hold these truths to be self evident . . ." he was giving us a starting point, as he did for the about-to-be-born American nation. Thomas Jefferson, like many of the founders, placed great faith in the writings of earlier thinkers including John Locke, who, in *An Essay Concerning Human Understanding*, laid out concepts that anticipated the idea of a Belief Window upon which we can write—and rewrite—what we believe to be true.

Locke defines the self as "that conscious thinking thing, (whatever substance, made up of whether spiritual, or material, simple, or compounded, it matters not) which is sensible, or conscious of pleasure and pain, capable of happiness or misery."

He goes on to remind us that we begin gathering and remembering our behavior-determining experiences early in life, and that childhood can do much to shape how we confront the world of the present. Locke also suggested that "the little and almost insensible impressions on our tender infancies have very important and lasting consequences." He makes the case that the "associations of ideas" (we could call them beliefs about things) that a person makes early in life are more important than those they make later because they are foundational concepts that will mold that person's life.

So if you are looking for some truths to write on your Belief Window, why not start with a look at the Declaration of Independence—life, liberty, the pursuit of happiness (and one of my own, equality of opportunity). These concepts are a great place to begin. And, in Locke's view, finding those unleashing truths early is better than finding them later.

Then continue your search, but remember the story of the young sapling oak growing beneath the shelter of the old oak. Don't wander too far afield until your roots and trunk and branches are well enough developed to withstand the inevitable onslaughts of life.

DUTY, HONOR, COUNTRY

As a teenager, I saw the movie *MacArthur*, starring the great actor Gregory Peck. The film moved me tremendously and started me on a path of studying this great general's life. I learned, first of all, that General Douglas MacArthur was a man of contradictions, filled with pride and humility, with arrogance and meekness, with both right and wrong principles on his Belief Window. But after much study, I concluded that on balance, he had some powerful principles on his window that would serve me well if they were rewritten on mine.

A few years ago, I was invited to speak at a conference at West Point, The United States Military Academy. I stayed at the hotel on base. Understanding that I not only was a huge fan of General MacArthur but also had named my son after him, the staff took me to visit the suite where General MacArthur's mother lived while he was a cadet at the Academy. While standing alone in the sitting area of that suite, I noticed the sun streaming across the wooded river banks and through the windows, and I could see in my mind's eye General MacArthur, the aged and bowed warrior, delivering his last great speech at the "Point" when he said:

> Duty, Honor, Country: Those three hallowed words reverently dictate what you ought to be, what you can be, what you will be. They are your rallying points: to build courage when courage seems to fail; to regain faith when there seems to be little cause for faith; to create hope when hope becomes forlorn.
>
> Unhappily, I possess neither that eloquence of diction, that poetry of imagination, nor that brilliance of metaphor to tell you all that they mean.
>
> The unbelievers will say they are but words, but a slogan, but a flamboyant phrase. Every pedant, every demagogue, every cynic, every hypocrite, every troublemaker, and I am sorry to say, some others of an entirely different character, will try to downgrade them even to the extent of mockery and ridicule.

> But these are some of the things they do. They build your basic character. They mold you for your future roles as the custodians of the nation's defense. They make you strong enough to know when you are weak, and brave enough to face yourself when you are afraid. They teach you to be proud and unbending in honest failure, but humble and gentle in success; not to substitute words for actions, not to seek the path of comfort, but to face the stress and spur of difficulty and challenge; to learn to stand up in the storm but to have compassion on those who fall; to master yourself before you seek to master others; to have a heart that is clean, a goal that is high; to learn to laugh, yet never forget how to weep; to reach into the future yet never neglect the past; to be serious yet never to take yourself too seriously; to be modest so that you will remember the simplicity of true greatness, the open mind of true wisdom, the meekness of true strength.
>
> They give you a temper of the will, a quality of the imagination, a vigor of the emotions, a freshness of the deep springs of life, a temperamental predominance of courage over timidity, of an appetite for adventure over love of ease. They create in your heart the sense of wonder, the unfailing hope of what next, and the joy and inspiration of life. They teach you in this way to be an officer and a gentleman.[3]

"They teach you . . . to be an officer and a gentleman." Some of you may have no desire to be known as an officer, but we should all, I believe, aspire at all times—particularly in the heat of challenging times—to truly be gentlemen and ladies.

And so I decided to add to my window: duty, honor, country, modesty, simplicity, an open mind, true wisdom, meekness, true strength, a vigor of emotion, imagination, a temperate approach, courage over timidity, an appetite for adventure, a sense of wonder, an unfailing hope of what comes next, a joy for and a searching for inspiration in life.

Take some time now to examine your own Belief Window with some of the tools and clearer lenses you have learned about in this chapter. Identify those beliefs that are not working for you, and list the beliefs that you would like to add to your window.

THE LENS: Key Principles to Remember

Francis Scott Key taught us . . .

YOU CAN SEE HOPE IN THE DARKEST NIGHT

- Francis Scott Key, held captive in a small boat in Baltimore Harbor, watched the aggressive British attack on Fort McHenry. He could have lost hope and feared for the worst, but he saw, "through the rockets red glare, the bombs bursting in air," the symbol of the Republic and the faith, hope and glorious future it represented.
- How we see things matters as much as what we see.

NOTES

1. John A. Widtsoe, *Evidences and Reconciliations* (Salt Lake City: Bookcraft, 1943), 20, 21.
2. C.S. Lewis, *Mere Christianity* (New York: HarperCollins, 2001), 3–4.
3. Douglas MacArthur, West Point, May 12, 1962.

Chapter III

THE LAW

CHANGING THE ENERGY DYNAMIC

Wars have an energy dynamic of their own, as initiative shifts back and forth between each side of the conflict, and the winter of 1777–78 was arguably the low point for the American colonists in their struggle to gain independence from Great Britain. Having failed to take Philadelphia from the north in 1776, the British had decided to attempt a southerly approach in the summer of 1777, and General George Washington was trying to second-guess their intended landing site.

After achieving a surprise landing at the head of Chesapeake Bay, British troops advanced toward Philadelphia while the Continental Army moved south to meet them. On September 11, the two armies met in battle at Brandywine Creek south of Philadelphia, where the British easily routed the less organized American troops. The bulk of the American army then retreated northward, while at the same time the Continental Congress abandoned Philadelphia and fled to York, seventy miles to the west.

As 1778 began, George Washington and his troops were shivering in the snows of their winter quarters at Valley Forge, northwest of Philadelphia. Thirty miles away, British officers and troops occupied the comfortable homes and government buildings of the young nation's capital, and the British fleet stood guard at the mouth of the Delaware River to control maritime access and ensure the flow of supplies to their troops in the occupied colonial city. To many observers at the time, the future of the American dream of independence looked bleak indeed.

While many Americans no doubt were pessimistic about their future at that particularly challenging time in the nation's history, one man was determined to change the dynamics of the situation. John Barry, a Scotsman who had emigrated to America, had been commissioned as a captain in the fledgling American Navy. In early 1776, while in command of the American ship *Lexington*, he defeated and captured a British ship, taking her to Philadelphia, the first English prize of war brought to that city. In December of 1776, Barry had helped transport George Washington and the Continental Army across the Delaware in the surprise attack on British and German soldiers in Trenton and Princeton recounted in chapter 1. But now, a year later, Barry found himself on land, awaiting the command of a frigate that was under construction.

After the British capture of Philadelphia in the autumn of 1777, John Barry served as the shore-based Senior Commander of the Navy at the Port of Philadelphia, operating from Bordentown, up the Delaware River from Philadelphia, where many of the American vessels had been moved to prevent them from falling into British hands. With an odd assortment of ships and small craft at his disposal, Barry set about to harass the British fleet blocking the lower Delaware River.

To the British, the irritating John Barry seemed to be everywhere. In October, part of his flotilla prevented the passage of the British fleet to Philadelphia, running two British frigates aground, one of which blew up when gunpowder on board exploded. Barry's forces saved several American ships on the Delaware River south of Philadelphia by successfully slipping them past the occupied city in the middle of the night of November 16, adding to the ragtag American flotilla to the north.

On Monday, January 5, 1778, Barry implemented the first of several innovative actions against the British that showed his ongoing determination to change the energy dynamic of the war during this particularly cold winter, when so much else seemed to go against the Americans. In one of Barry's attempts to harass and destroy the enemy ships anchored in the Delaware River off Philadelphia, the British in the occupied capital were surprised to see what appeared to be a number of ships' buoys floating down the river toward them. The "buoys" were actually kegs filled with gunpowder, and when fired upon by the British batteries, they exploded. The event soon became known as the "Battle of the Kegs." In the words of a humorous ditty composed by patriot Francis Hopkinson,

> The cannons roar from shore to shore,
> The small arms make a rattle;
> Since war's began, I'm sure no man
> E'er saw so strange a battle.[1]

In early March, Captain Barry went after the British fleet again. This time he assembled a waterborne assortment of rowboats and barges and, according to some accounts, mounted cannons on their bows. Some thought the idea of arming and sending what some derisively called "washtubs" against armed ships was foolish and certain to fail. But John Barry was confident he could do it, and he proved to be right.

Barry filled the boats with twenty-seven men armed with rifles, swords, and boarding hooks and set off down the Delaware with muffled oars. His "washtubs" came upon two transport ships from Rhode Island, both laden with supplies intended for the British. The two unarmed ships were boarded without a fight and quickly captured.

Barry's washtub warriors then removed the supplies to the New Jersey shore and sent them overland to the Continental Army and other American forces. They later burned the two ships, so they would be of no value to the enemy.

While still engaged in the encounter with the supply vessels, Barry and his crews turned to face an armed British schooner approaching the scene. He sent an armed group with orders for the schooner to surrender, which surprisingly it did. They took the captain, officers, and crew as prisoners. The schooner also yielded supplies and important documents relating to the British forces. Captain Barry sent these items, together with cheese and a jar of pickled oysters, to General Washington—with the note that they had come from a store of wine and luxuries intended for the Philadelphia table of General Howe, the British army commander.

The news of "Barry's Boats" and the captured ships and supplies made John Barry an instant hero, boosting American morale at a critical time in the Revolutionary War. On March 12, four days after the battle on the river, General George Washington wrote a letter of commendation to John Barry, congratulating him on "the success that has crowned your gallantry and address in the late attacks on the enemy's ships." In his conclusion, Washington said, "May a suitable recompense always attend your bravery."[2]

Martin Griffin, who wrote an exhaustive biography of John Barry, summarizes the results of Barry's actions, which shifted the dynamics of the challenging situation he and his nation faced during a crucial period in a dark chapter in American history:

> Barry with twenty-seven men had captured one major, two captains, three lieutenants, ten soldiers and one hundred seamen and marines. . . . He captured also many letters and official papers. . . . Barry's success won the admiration of friend and foe. It was at this time Sir William Howe is said to have offered Captain Barry [who had originally come to America from Scotland] twenty thousand guineas

and the command of a British frigate if he would desert the service of the United Colonies. The alleged answer of Barry is stated to have been: "Not the value and command of the whole British fleet can seduce me from the cause of my country."[3]

John Barry served with distinction through the remainder of the Revolution, including several hard-won victories in battles at sea. After the war, he became the senior commander of the navy of the young United States, in which post he served until his death in 1803. He is known today as the father of the US Navy.

Of Barry's exploits on the Delaware River in the winter of 1778, a modern commentator has written:

> It's easy to become discouraged when the storms of life bring misfortune or distress. But Captain John Barry knew that adversity often opens the door of opportunity. He recognized it, acted on it, and, as a result, became a national hero.
>
> From him and many others like him we learn an important lesson: Often the very adversity that plagues our lives is, in disguise, an opportunity for greatness.[4]

THE LAWS OF PHYSICS AND AN "AHA" ABOUT ENERGY

I took just enough chemistry and physics in college to be dangerous. In particular, I was fascinated with all of the "laws" that scientists have identified that explain the phenomena of the natural world. I have called this chapter "The Law" because it is my own extrapolation of one basic law physicists call the Law of the Conservation of Energy. This law states that *energy cannot be created or destroyed, but can change its form*. The idea that energy "can change its form" jumped out at me. In studying this particular law, I realized that it applied far beyond the study of physics.

I am not a chemist or a physicist, and I certainly am no medical doctor. So, I base my proposal on personal experience and observation of patterns around me, not on specialized education or academic insight. While I approach the subject practically, I have shared my insights with academic experts in the above-mentioned fields and have found among them some resonance with this approach for confronting and conquering challenging times.

In my own life I have found that a day's labor, hard won, leaves me exhausted, not just in the physical sense but also emotionally, spiritually, and mentally. When I used to work on the family farm bailing and stacking hay, I learned what physical exhaustion felt like. I have since learned that, for me at least, mental, emotional, and spiritual exhaustion can be even more profound than the physical kind. I have also learned that retreat and renewal can, if properly done, restore the energy that was consumed in earlier battles, including "labors of love."

I have always found it fascinating that the leaders of three of the world's great religions understood and practiced the law of renewal. The Buddha would retreat to meditate under a tree in what we now call northern India—a site, I understand, still venerated by the followers of this holy personage. In Islam, the Quran contains numerous accounts of the Prophet retreating to a cave to be instructed, guided, and uplifted by the Angel Gabriel. And, in Christianity, Christ frequently retreated from the pressing masses at Galilee to meditate, pray, and prepare in the wilderness.

Physical energy is always undergoing transfer and change. Our bodies literally store energy that originated from the sun's heat and was then transformed through photosynthesis in plants into a form that animals can store and utilize. Our store of energy comes from foods derived from plants and animals, and it is depleted in the form of heat generated by our muscles and other bodily processes, which is then released into the atmosphere around us.

When I get a good night's sleep and watch my diet, I find that I more easily recapture lost physical energy. The same thing goes for mental and spiritual energy. When I live my values, repent of my weaknesses, and seek to do good, I restore lost spiritual vigor. And when I rest my mind and feed it quality food instead of a diet of mass market mental junk, my mind responds with increased energy and renewed commitment to move forward.

DIRECTION OF ENERGY—CHANGING ITS FORM

Properly renewed by infusions of nourishing physical and mental food, we can restore energy that initially seemed lost or destroyed. When you wake in the morning with these various energies replenished, you are ready to confront and conquer the challenges of the day. Effective speaking and teaching can be exhausting, and people sometimes ask me how I have so much energy in those situations. I am sure some of it is genetic and some the consequence of the habits just discussed, but I have come to realize that a lot of my energy comes in just making the choice to be energized.

When I was a young boy, my father would wake us, often very early because for us there were chores to do. (He seemed to relish this activity most on Saturdays for some reason.) My father's wake-up call was his own vocal rendition of the reveille bugle call, with words added: "It's time to get up, it's time to get up, it's time to get up this morning." Some days I found myself under the covers, muttering under his continued singing: "Some day you're going to murder the bugler, spend the rest of your life, the rest of your life in bed." Don't think for a minute that I didn't find the phrase about "murdering the bugler" to be the most attractive part of the awakening!

Still, I did learn how to get up and fully engage the day. We engage the day by making choices—choices about our newly renewed energies. Here is what I think goes on right from the start of any day:

At the beginning of the day, we have a choice. All of our energy—mental, physical, emotional, or spiritual—needs to go somewhere, and life offers it at least two paths. We can send this jealously guarded and carefully replenished energy down a negative channel, where it will come out as complaints, manipulation, and procrastination. Or, we can choose instead a positive, productive channel called adapting, influencing, and acting. We'll talk more about this in the next chapter.

We determine the quality of our lives, I believe, by our answers to these two questions:

1. Will I develop the habits, discipline, and actions that restore lost energy?
2. Will I channel that restored energy down positive paths?

In challenging times, when things aren't working out exactly as desired or planned, the choice to reenergize and to channel positively has a great effect on how things turn out for you and others. Challenging times may find us wasting precious energy if we are not careful. When we fail to exert the discipline necessary to change the energy dynamic, to restore and regain consumed or lost energy, we make our first mistake. If we then use up all of our energy in negative channeling, we can turn ourselves into defeated observers of our own demise. Taking hard-won energy and channeling it in a negative way is a pitiful form of personal waste and lost individual and public opportunity.

You will not likely be called to steer a tiny craft into the face of a fleet of fearsome men-o'-war, as did John Barry in the challenging winter of 1777–78. But you may well be asked to confront other looming challenges. With a store of energy, rightly directed, you can come off conqueror.

THE LAW: Key Principles to Remember

John Barry taught us . . .

IF YOU HAVE NOTHING ELSE, YOU HAVE ENERGY

- Tasked with the responsibility to push the British fleet back into the Atlantic and lacking any resources other than his own energy, ingenuity and a handful of starving, cold men, John Barry attacked, damaged and pushed the British back, protecting the American troops to fight another day.
- Learning how to create and direct our own energy and how to inspire others to do the same can create the resources necessary, even in challenging times where resources are short or non-existent, to do great things.

NOTES

1. Martin I.J. Griffin, *The Story of Commodore John Barry* (Philadelphia, 1908), 16.
2. Ibid., 18.
3. Ibid.
4. Lloyd D. Newell, "The Door of Opportunity," *Music and the Spoken Word*, program #4099.

Chapter IV

THE LANDSCAPE

In the course of a year, I spend more time on airplanes than I would like. I have devised a number of ways to make good use of that time. I read, work on my laptop, listen to good music, and sometimes just put on the earphones and sleep.

Once in a great while, when the weather is just right, I find myself looking out the window. Sometimes we pass through canyons of towering and majestic clouds, brilliant on the sunward side and warm gray in the shadows. On other occasions, I find myself looking down at the parade of mountains, plains, woodlands, great rivers, and lakes that glide by below. The American landscape is a vast canvas, with striking contrasts in terrain and color. The land and patterns of human habitation form an endless procession on a transcontinental flight—the great cities of the eastern corridor; the forested mountains of the Appalachian range; the checkered fields of the great plains, the abrupt rise of the snowcapped Rockies; the mazes, brilliant sandstone buttes, and tablelands of the Colorado Plateau and the intermountain desert; the towering Sierra Nevada and dormant volcanoes of the Cascades; and finally, the surf of the Pacific Ocean.

In looking at the world, you can take a physical perspective and see mountains, hills, deserts, savannas, rivers, forests, streams, and seas.

You can also make connections between the attributes of the physical world and human interactions. Among these are the analogies about mountains and molehills, smooth sailing and rough seas, deluges and droughts—attributes of the physical world that we apply to the ways people view and approach challenges. Another common aspect of the human landscape is how we tend to see things in dichotomies—them or us, good or bad, for us or against us, right or wrong, easy or difficult. These analogies present a sample of the ways in which we tend to see the world of human interactions.

For myself, the array of dichotomies is interesting, but the dichotomies don't always help me find solutions to the opportunities and challenges that come with both human interaction as well as interaction with the physical world. But the lessons of experience have helped me find a simple and practical way to look at the world—one that helps me move in a positive direction, even in difficult circumstances. The idea is fairly simple; I mentally divide the human landscape of the world and its situations and events into three broad categories:

1. Situations and things over which I have *no control,*
2. Situations and things over which I have *some control,* and
3. Situations and things over which I have *total control.*

Now, admittedly these categories are broad and you can push on my approach enough to cause it to be inappropriate or to fail in some situations, but for practical purposes, I have found value in this perspective.

Each of the three levels of control requires a different approach, especially in the most difficult or challenging situations. Within each level, I see two opposing choices:

In a situation when I have . . .	**I can either . . .**
No Control	Adapt or Murmur/Lament
Some Control	Influence or Manipulate
Total Control	Act or Procrastinate

Notice that the behavior options in each of these kinds of situations include a choice between a positive behavior and an opposite negative behavior. In my experience, the first, or positive, options (adapt, influence, or act) have the greatest potential to meet my needs over time (remember the key question of the Reality Model). But I also recognize in myself (and many others) a strong pull toward the negative options—murmuring/lamenting, manipulating, or procrastinating. Interestingly, all three of these negative behavior choices contribute little or nothing to solve a challenging or dangerous situation in ways that produce good results over time. I find that my personal challenge is to try to minimize or eliminate the second category of behaviors and to focus on and use the first category more often—if not always.

In teaching this concept to others, I have found people tend to want to create static lists of specific behaviors related to each degree of control. Although such lists have some value, I think a better approach is to learn to use this model to drive two questions.

Question One: How much control do I have here (no, some, total)?
Question Two: Which response will best meet my needs over time (adapt, influence, act)?

Then, having tried to honestly assess and answer each question, I try to implement the response in practical terms. A personal example:

Early in our marriage, when I was a college student holding down three jobs, and my wife Heather was fully engaged with the bulk of the task of raising our two children, we often had money problems. After some trial and error, we came to approach our challenge by asking and answering the two questions:

Question One: How much control do we have here?

Answers:

- No control over the fact that we need money now
- Some control over how we get it
- Total control over not getting in this mess again

Question Two: Which response will best meet our needs over time?

Answers:

- Adapt—borrow what we need to correct the immediate problem.
- Influence—convince my bosses to let me work extra hours (I had some very considerate employers)
- Act—eliminate or more carefully manage our expenses in the future

And, although things didn't always work out exactly as planned, we made the exciting discovery that things often did work out nearly as planned. We had found a simple and practical way to more clearly identify challenging situations and confront and conquer them.

In addition to providing a structured way to view problems at the individual and small group level, this model for responding to challenging situations can work with large-scale challenges as well. What many historians say was one of the most challenging and crucial events in World War II provides a powerful example of using this approach to deal with complex and difficult situations.

By the end of 1943, the war was more than four years old, and Nazi Germany had conquered and occupied most of continental Europe. The tide of the war had been turned a year earlier in Russia and North Africa, but the conflict was far from over. American and British armies were bogged down in a near stalemate in Italy, with German forces contesting every inch of territory as the Allies pressed northward. Russian troops were slowly but steadily advancing toward Germany from the east, and in England, a great assemblage of men, aircraft, tanks, and other war matériel was being brought together for an invasion across the English Channel into Nazi-occupied France.

The landing of 150,000 Allied troops on the French coast in June of 1944 would be the climax of more than two years of enormous preparations involving thousands of decisions. As the target date drew near, the success or failure of the invasion increasingly hinged on a few critical factors and the life-and-death decisions that would need to be made about them.

Realizing that the Allies were likely to attempt landings in occupied France, the Germans had fortified much of the French coast. In a giant intelligence game, both Allies and Germans tried to second-guess each other. The Allies sought to determine the location and nature of German defenses and forces along the French side of the English Channel. The Germans tried to identify where along one hundred fifty miles of French coastline the Allies would attempt to land.

In England, American General Dwight D. Eisenhower, the Supreme Allied Commander of OVERLORD (the code name for the assault), considered all of the incoming information and faced some supremely daunting, difficult, and critically vital choices. They knew that the planned D-Day landings on the beaches of Normandy could change the dynamic of the war in the Allies' favor or they could result in horrific short-term casualties and great loss of life over the long term.

By late May 1944, plans had been finalized. The troops had been trained for their missions and stood by for orders to proceed. A mighty armada of warships, cargo ships, and troopships crowded the ports of southern England, ready to depart on a moment's notice. Fighter squadrons, bombers, and transport aircraft were on full alert, awaiting the command to leave on aerial support missions across the channel. The stage was set for what would be one of the largest single military operations ever undertaken in the history of the world.

As described by historian Stephen A. Ambrose in *The Supreme Commander*, the immediate goal had been set: "the main thrust of OVERLORD was to get ashore and stay. This goal affected every decision."[1]

Having established that goal, General Eisenhower and his commanders had to begin dealing with realities—a vast number of situations and circumstances over which they would have no control, some control, or total control.

Ambrose continues,

> [The assault] had to come at low tide, because the German defenses were built around steel obstacles that covered the area of the beach between the high- and low-water marks. The obstacles, often capped with Teller mines, would rip the belly out of any landing craft that passed over them. By landing at low tide, the Allies would have to cross an unprotected beach under German fire, but that was preferable to drowning in sinking landing craft.[2]

The timing of the invasion was the first of several major "no control" factors Eisenhower had to consider. In order for the troops to get ashore and stay, low tide had to occur at or near the dawn because the armada of ships needed the darkness of night to travel undetected across the English Channel. During the spring of 1944, the needed tidal conditions on the Normandy beaches would occur only three times—during the first few days of May as well as the first and third weeks of June. The need for low tide at daybreak on the appointed day determined the timing of the assault, scheduled for the first week in June.

NO CONTROL: ADAPTING

After determining the possible landing dates, General Eisenhower and his planners turned to choosing where along the French coast to land the troops, a decision that offered few choices, none of them ideal. The Germans had fortified and built barriers and traps along every possible beach where a landing might be attempted. But Allied intelligence indicated that the Germans believed the attack would come at the narrowest part of the English Channel, between Dover and Calais. Allied counterintelligence efforts had successfully diverted attention to this location by using fake radio transmissions suggesting major military activity near Dover. Aware of the resulting German expectations, the Allied command selected the Normandy beaches one hundred fifty miles to the west as the best landing location along the channel coast, the area likely to have the fewest German troops and fortifications.

As it always is, weather on the projected day of the invasion was a definite "no control" factor. Eisenhower faced the challenge not only of adapting to the realities of the landing place and time but also of dealing with the "chance" card of whatever the weather offered on the selected day. All of these interwoven factors had to be considered so that the overall goal to "get ashore and stay" would not be put at risk.

In a world offering various levels of control, great leaders find ways to accomplish what they need to accomplish—even in the most challenging times and circumstances. In this particular case, Eisenhower reminded his generals: "Every obstacle must be overcome, every inconvenience suffered and every risk run to ensure that our blow is decisive. We cannot afford to fail."[3]

SOME CONTROL: INFLUENCING

One of Eisenhower's greatest challenges was managing the tremendous expectations and egos of his primary team and his bosses. People like American President Franklin D. Roosevelt, British Prime Minister Winston Churchill, and French General Charles de Gaulle all had their own clear ideas about the form the invasion should take, as did British General Bernard Montgomery, American Chief of Staff George Marshall, and others. In working with these and other complex and talented individuals, Eisenhower had—unlike his lack of control over the weather, timing, and location of the invasion—some control over outcomes. He made the most of his opportunity to influence and deal effectively with all of the differing personalities whose support and help he needed in order to ensure the success of the Normandy invasion. As Ambrose explains:

> Precisely because of Eisenhower's personality, he was by all odds the best of the British or American officers available to deal with the

> French. De Gaulle liked, respected and counted on him heavily. . . . All these relationships, and the many others involved in the position Eisenhower was assuming, had innumerable ramifications and complex interactions. Doing something to satisfy Montgomery might make [General George] Patton angry; a decision that pleased Marshall would leave [Field Marshal Alan] Brooke unhappy; bowing to the President's wishes could mean opposing the Prime Minister. The Supreme Commander would have to be able to maintain a balance and still defeat the Germans. Eisenhower was aware of the complexities.[4]

Finding agreement among this cast of international players, all with their own views, egos, and ideas about what should be done, was perhaps the greatest challenge Eisenhower faced during the months leading up to D-Day. Because of his personal integrity and proven ability to see best solutions among the many offered, he was able to influence the leaders mentioned above, his peers as well as his superiors and subordinates. From his personal integrity and previous successes in battle, he had gained their trust and was able to win support for his ideas.

TOTAL CONTROL: ACTING

"By the last week in May, Eisenhower felt he had met and dealt with all the problems in his power to settle," Ambrose reports. "The number of unknowns were still large, but there was nothing he could do about them."[5]

Even knowing rationally that we are as prepared as we can be in difficult situations, we must never underestimate the emotional pressures of less than perfect situations, especially on moral and well-meaning people. As D-Day neared, the British general who was chief of air operations for OVERLORD decided that the drop zones in one of the sectors were not suitable for landing the troop gliders that were part of the invasion force. He predicted the "futile slaughter of two fine divisions" of troops, with losses as much as 70 percent.

As Eisenhower later put it, "It would be difficult to conceive of a more soul-racking problem." Ambrose describes the decision Eisenhower faced: "If he cancelled the airborne operation he would have to cancel the landing at Utah [Beach], which would in turn disrupt all the plans. . . . [He] went to the telephone, and told [the chief of air operations] that the operation would go ahead as scheduled."[6]

By the morning of June 3, weather reports seemed to be favorable, but changes appeared to be in the offing, and confusion surfaced among the weather forecasters as to what the weather would be on D-Day, planned for Monday, June 5. Eisenhower alone had the responsibility of sorting out the conflicting weather reports and making the decision to proceed with the invasion or call it off. While Eisenhower had no control over the weather, he did have total control over whether or not the invasion should proceed.

On Sunday, June 4, a strong storm blew in from the northwest, and Eisenhower decided to postpone the invasion for one day, to Tuesday, June 6. To delay beyond that would have essentially meant aborting the entire operation. On Eisenhower's orders, preparations were put on hold, and aerial and naval forces were directed to stand down. Everyone waited on the weather and the general's final decision about Tuesday.

After dinner on the evening of June 4, Eisenhower found himself in a conversation with his team about the looming question: "go" or "no go." Ambrose describes the events that led to the final decision:

> If there was going to be an invasion before June 19 [the next date the timing of low tide would be favorable], Eisenhower had to decide now. [General Walter Bedell] Smith [Eisenhower's Chief of Staff] was struck by the loneliness and isolation of a commander at a time when such a momentous decision was to be taken by him, with full knowledge that failure or success rests on the individual decision. Looking out at the wind-driven rain . . . Eisenhower calmly weighed the

> alternatives, and at 9:45 p.m. said, "I am quite positive that the order must be given."[7]

Despite the fact that it was still raining, orders were given to the fleets to stand by and be ready to sail, with instructions that a final go-ahead for the invasion would come before dawn.

Eisenhower tossed and turned that night, finally arising at 3:30 a.m. on Monday, June 5. The weather appeared to be turning for the better but still would not be ideal. If he were to call off the attack, he must do so now, before ships and men began moving the one hundred miles across the channel, at which point they would lose the element of surprise and recall would be next to impossible. Eisenhower reviewed the weather data, thought for a moment, and then, in Ambrose's account, "said quietly but clearly, 'O.K. let's go.'"[8]

The aircraft were loaded and readied for takeoff. The warships and transports prepared to leave their ports, and those standing by in the English Channel resumed their course toward their assembly positions. Before the dawn of June 6, D-Day, the mightiest armada ever assembled was in position off the Normandy coast. At daybreak the first waves of the invasion launched and secured a foothold on the beach. More than 150,000 men and their implements of war poured into occupied France. The tide of World War II quickly turned toward victory for the Allies, which came with the total defeat and surrender of Nazi Germany less than a year later.

As British scientist Sir Isaac Newton penned, "Knowledge is power." Having correct knowledge is essential in making choices in no control, some control, and total control situations. Our world is filled not only with challenge but also with vast quantities of information from millions of sources of varying quality and reliability. It has also been said, "Wisdom is knowledge rightfully applied." The fine line between a bad decision and a good one—between "O.K. let's go" and "maybe we should wait"—is more blurry and ephemeral than you might like. Yet execution of decisions is still the critical skill for dealing with challenging times.

In the next three chapters, we will take a closer look at how leaders and everyday people in the past and present have dealt with challenging situations over which they had no control, some control, or total control—and the results of the decisions they made.

THE LANDSCAPE: Key Principles to Remember

General Dwight Eisenhower taught us . . .

TO KNOW THE LANDSCAPE BEFORE WE CREATE AND LAUNCH OUR PLAN

- General Eisenhower, responsible for one of the greatest military battles in history, bore a commander's burden never heard of before or since. He met this great challenge by examining the physical and human landscape and . . .
  - First, determining the key factors and whether he had total control, some control or no control over them, and
  - Second, choosing to adapt rather than murmur, influence rather than manipulate, act rather than procrastinate. In doing so, Eisenhower defeated an evil enemy and saved the cause of freedom.

NOTES

1. Stephen E. Ambrose, *The Supreme Commander: The War Years of General Dwight D. Eisenhower* (New York: Doubleday, 1970), 331.

2. Ibid., 333.
3. Ibid., 337.
4. Ibid., 323.
5. Ibid., 406.
6. Ibid., 407.
7. Ibid., 416.
8. Ibid.

Chapter V

THE LION

A plaque on my desk at home contains the following thought, a partial quote taken from the book of Proverbs in the Old Testament:

"The [fearful] man saith, There is a lion in the way" (Proverbs 26:13).

In our lives we often find lions that stand in the way of our progress. Considering the levels of control discussed in the preceding chapter—no control, some control, and total control situations—the "lion in the way" is a metaphor representing challenges over which we have no control or, at best, very little control. In these troubled times, the lion could be the loss of your job or inability to secure needed credit for your business. Or it may be a long-held belief that is keeping you from moving ahead positively in a relationship or other aspects of your personal life. It may be lack of skills or certification that are keeping you from advancing in your career. It may be an unexpected event that drastically alters your vision of the future. In almost all of these or other similar "lion in the way" situations, you have a choice to make. These challenges require us to adapt or work with the situation as best we can if we are to move beyond the lion and achieve our goals.

ADAPT—THE NO CONTROL CHOICE

The choice to adapt when dealing with a lion is not about learning to live with something we wish could change. And it is certainly not about giving up or giving in, although there may be some lions, such as discovering a life-threatening medical condition, that we feel totally powerless to do anything about. It is about finding a way over, under, around, or through the lion.

Too often we waste precious energy on the negative twin to adapting—lamenting or murmuring while doing nothing about the lion—when we could be using that energy to find a better way around it. When we murmur or lament, we consume energy—physical, emotional, mental, and spiritual energy. But that energy does nothing to move the lion or solve the situation.

In challenging times, you will encounter many things over which you have little or no control. Learning to channel your energy into adapting rather than murmuring has the greatest potential to move you forward and impact your situation or the larger world in ways you care about. In many cases, you may feel that just living with the status quo in a no control or low control situation will not do. You may also find more ways around the lions in your life than you might realize.

A few years ago, a good friend of mine, after living with near-perfect health for more than sixty years, was diagnosed with a progressively degenerative neuromuscular disease. It has a fancy medical name, but neither its cause nor a cure has yet been found. The disease has gradually weakened my friend's upper arm and shoulder muscles, along with his thigh and abdominal muscles. The days of enjoying hiking and taking long walks have come to an end as his diminishing muscle strength has reduced his stamina and made uphill walking difficult, even on a gentle grade. Lifting heavy objects is out of the question. Simple motions such as reaching for food across a dinner table can be tricky.

Just negotiating the normal terrain of life often requires my friend to use a walking stick or physical help from others. Balance has become affected, requiring care in maintaining equilibrium on uneven surfaces or ice and snow. Stairs that my friend used to take two at a time now require concentration and careful movement, and he has gained a special degree of gratitude for handrails. Even air travel has become a challenge, especially if traveling alone. Putting things into the overhead bins is impossible, and getting into or out of an airline seat requires careful maneuvering to get help from muscles that aren't affected by his condition. Getting on board an aircraft without a boarding ramp is almost impossible because of the steep stairs used to board off the tarmac.

My friend could have encountered this lion, looked at the obstacles and dangers and uncertainties that the lion presented, and murmured, lamented, or given up. Although there were moments of lament, he didn't give up. As I talked with him about how he gets around this life-changing lion, he responded: "At first, I was starting to let myself fall into the 'why me?' and 'why now?' self-pity mode. But as things have gradually gotten worse, I find my mind automatically searching for and implementing different 'work-arounds,' as I have come to call them." My friend has found ways to continue working in his profession from home, and he finds satisfaction in the kind of work he does. "I've even come up with work-arounds that enable me to paint and pursue my lifelong interest in art," he continued. "I can't hike anymore, but I've found ways to get out and enjoy the outdoors, and we still take road trips to favorite places."

My friend's philosophy in all this is simple. In his words: "Rather than worry about what I can't do, I'm grateful for all the things I still *can* do." When he encounters a new limitation arising from his situation, he almost subconsciously sets out to find a work-around, whether involving the remaining healthy muscles or finding other ways to accomplish what he needs to do. In most cases, he's been successful. And even though the boundaries of his physical world have, of necessity, slowly closed in around him these past several years, he feels that life is still good.

The reason our minds tend to find a work-around rather than give in when confronted with a no control or low control situation lies in a fundamental human characteristic that I suspect is part of the human DNA. It may have something to do with the survival instinct that drives much of human behavior, that inner strength and determination that enabled people to survive in the Nazi concentration camps of World War II. Something in human nature can't or won't accept the status quo. Our inner self demands that it change—there simply must *be* a way and we must *find* a way.

DEALING WITH LIONS ON THE BATTLEFIELD

In an instant, soldiers, sailors, and airmen in the front lines of combat can find themselves facing very dangerous lions in situations where they truly have no choice but to respond. Often without warning, they are thrown by the winds of chance into life-threatening situations. In such cases, the only choice these men and women have is to adapt to the situation or die. Merely lamenting or murmuring is not an option.

Staff Sergeant Christopher Bain, an Army reservist from Baltimore, Maryland, served in Iraq in 2004 as a reconnaissance and chemical weapons specialist. Jonathan Weisman included Bain's story, a 2006 interview, in a series of firsthand accounts featured in *The Washington Post*. Sergeant Bain's experience was not one of facing a great gun battle with many armed enemies, tanks, and artillery. Instead, his story represents the typical kind of random attack by small hidden bands of insurgents that could occur any time to any American combat group, almost anywhere in Iraq.

Sergeant Bain described one particular day as the "best and worst day" of his four-month tour in Iraq. Having just enjoyed a chance reunion with his identical twin brother in a visit to another Army post, he returned to his own unit at Al Taji. Upon arrival, he and his squad received orders for another convoy mission.

Even before the squad left their base, they came under fire from mortars hidden outside the base's perimeter. In Sergeant Bain's words:

> There were four to six of them. They hit us with small arms around 5:30 or 6 pm. The sun was going down . . . I was hearing mortar fire, and I asked if it was all outgoing. It took about 50 seconds for the first round to hit, about 50 meters in front of us. We jumped out, throwing people under cover for protection. I just stayed out there too long, making sure my guys were protected.[1]

After he had helped a soldier with a broken arm get under the truck, a mortar round landed three feet in front of Sergeant Bain. Shrapnel from the explosion ripped into his left forearm. Then he took a rifle round in his right elbow but was still somehow able to get himself beneath the truck.

> I can tell you second by second. It comes back to me every day. All I saw was all the blood. I was under a truck and just gushing. . . . I'm lucky I didn't bleed out. With all the adrenaline and all, I didn't feel my arm. I was crying over my finger. [His ring finger had nearly been severed by the blast.] Everything was like slow motion. I saw a medic. He was going "What hurts?" I couldn't hear him but I read his lips. . . . I said, "My finger, it's killing me." He said, "Your finger? Have you seen your arm?" I said, "What's wrong with my arm?"[2]

Within five days, Sergeant Bain was in Washington, DC, lying in a bed in Walter Reed Army Hospital. After months of surgery and treatment, he was left with irreparable nerve damage in his right arm. He couldn't feel anything with half of his right hand. The left hand could make a fist but could not do much else. The surgeons sewed his ring finger back on. He has short-term memory problems and carries a calendar and notepad with him so he can jot down things he needs to remember.

In confronting a very angry, raging lion that day in Iraq, Sergeant Bain's training and instinctive actions helped him adapt to the situation presented by the lion—not simply adapt, but adapt quickly. Like thousands of other wounded veterans of Iraq and other wars, Sergeant Bain has had to confront another lion—some serious and permanent disabilities—that will remain with him through his life. Yet even facing this unwelcome and ever-present lion, he could say, two years after the attack, "I'm not going to get any worse at this point. I'm not going to get any better. And I'm happy with it. My morale is still high. I wanted to go back, but they won't let me."[3]

After his injuries, Sergeant Christopher Bain was awarded a Purple Heart and honored in 2005 at a special "Salute to Heroes" event sponsored by the American Legion in Washington, DC. At this event, which Bain attended while still recovering from his injuries, President George W. Bush paid tribute to Bain and a number of other wounded veterans. Bain exhibited the same optimism he seemed to maintain through his long ordeal.

A LARGE LION BLOCKING THE WAY OF AN ENTIRE NATION

Some of the lions "in the way" not only block the way of individuals, but also present barriers that affect entire nations. While a student at Morehouse College in 1946, a young Martin Luther King Jr. wrote a letter to the *Atlanta Constitution.* Eight years before the Supreme Court's Brown v. Board of Education ruling gave birth to the activism of the 1950s and 1960s, the future civil rights leader was already beginning to take the measure of the large lion that lay in his and the American people's path. In his letter, he laid out the goals that would form the foundation of the movement he would eventually lead:

> We want and are entitled to the basic rights and opportunities of American citizens: The right to earn a living at work for which we are

> fitted by training and ability; equal opportunities in education, health, recreation, and similar public services; the right to vote; equality before the law; some of the same courtesy and good manners that we ourselves bring to human relations.[4]

These words demonstrate the intelligence and the passion of this young crusader, channeled into righteous indignation at the massive lion that blocked the way of all American people. The future Dr. King was right in 1946; he knew he was right, and he knew things must change. And he understood this truth almost two decades before he led the March on Washington. As history has shown, he would not relent. He would find his way over, around, or through this lion.

In reading Dr. King's autobiography, I am struck by his ability to identify new and creative channels to move the work forward. In the chapter he titled "The Sit-In Movement," he identifies numerous nonviolent methods of adapting in ways that could eliminate or at least mitigate the lion's presence:

> In 1960 an electrifying movement of Negro students shattered the placid surface of campuses and communities across the South. The young students of the South, through sit-ins and other demonstrations, gave America a glowing example of disciplined, dignified nonviolent action against the system of segregation. . . .
>
> I felt we had to continue to challenge the system of segregation, whether it was in the schools, public parks, church, lunch counters, or public libraries. Segregation had to be removed from our society. And Negroes had to be prepared to suffer, sacrifice and even die to gain their goals. We could not rest until we had achieved the ideals of our democracy. I prayed much over our Southern situation, and I came to the conclusion that we were in for a season of suffering.[5]

When, in December of 1961, the eleven so-called Freedom Riders arrived in Albany, Georgia, the adapting continued—still driving toward Dr. King's ultimate goal of ending segregation:

> Negroes, wielding nonviolent protest in its most creative utilization to date, challenged discrimination in public places. . . . On that broad front, the Albany Movement used all the methods of nonviolence: direct action expressed through mass demonstrations; jail-ins; sit-ins; wade-ins; and kneel-ins; political action; boycotts and legal actions. . . . In no other city of the deep South had all those methods of nonviolence been simultaneously exercised.[6]

Remember, adapting is not waiting around for others to do something. Nor is it about giving in and sitting at home in a soup of complaint and misery. Adapting means finding a way around the lion. Unfortunately, finding a way around large lions often can't be done without suffering some personal sacrifice.

On December 16, 1961, the Negro community of Albany, Georgia, made its stride toward freedom. Citizens from every quarter of the community made their moral witness against the system of segregation. They willingly went to jail to create an effective protest:

> I shall never forget the experience of seeing women over seventy, teenagers, and middle-aged adults—some with professional degrees in medicine, law, and education, some simple housekeepers and laborers—crowding the cells. This development was an indication that the Negro would not rest until all the barriers of segregation were broken down.[7]

You may not have to face the lion of segregation and discrimination, and you may or may not be over seventy, a teenager, or a middle-aged adult with a professional degree, or a housekeeper or laborer. But as you confront this challenging world, what lions do you face? Which of those lions do you feel so deeply about that you know in your soul that the situation must be overcome, that some way must be found to move forward?

If you find yourself facing lions over which you have little or no control, don't waste your valuable energy in complaint and misery, but rise up, adapt as much as is absolutely necessary, and put your energies toward finding a way around the lions that block your path.

SOME LIONS ARE NOT WHAT YOU THINK

Remember, not all lions in the way are necessarily something terrible, destructive, evil, or ferocious. Sometimes a lion that seems to be blocking your way is a blessing in disguise, becoming an obstacle that in the end strengthens you and actually helps you reach the goal toward which you are striving. And some lions may point you to another path you really should be following. In such cases, the lion is not what it first appears to be.

A passage in C.S. Lewis's *Chronicles of Narnia: The Silver Chair* beautifully tells about a thirsty little girl encountering the lion Aslan, who lies across the path, between the girl and a stream of fresh water. Lewis's description of the encounter offers much for us to think about:

> "Are you not thirsty?" said the Lion.
>
> "I'm dying of thirst," said Jill.
>
> "Then drink," said the Lion.
>
> "May I—could I—would you mind going away while I do?" said Jill.
>
> The Lion answered this only by a look and a very low growl. And as Jill gazed at its motionless bulk, she realized that she might as well have asked the whole mountain to move aside for her convenience.
>
> The delicious rippling noise of the stream was driving her nearly frantic. . . .
>
> "I daren't come and drink," said Jill.
>
> "Then you will die of thirst," said the Lion.
>
> "Oh dear!" said Jill coming another step nearer. "I suppose I must go and look for another stream then."
>
> "There is no other stream," said the Lion.
>
> It had never occurred to Jill to disbelieve the Lion—no one who had seen his stern face could do that—and her mind suddenly made itself up. It was the worst thing she had ever had to do, but she went

forward to the stream, knelt down, and began scooping up water in her hand. It was the coldest, most refreshing water she had ever tasted.[8]

THE LION: Key Principles to Remember

Dr. Martin Luther King, Jr. taught us . . .

WHEN YOU MEET RESISTANCE, EVEN OF A SUBSTANTIAL AND OVERWHELMING NATURE, STAY ON FOCUS AND FIND A WAY FORWARD

- Many of the forces of American society—the Army, National Guard, police forces, and the general population of the country—were, for most of his life, firmly aligned against Dr. King and committed to his personal defeat and the defeat of his dream. But he would not be swayed from his mission. He adapted to move through this field of resistance, but he never wavered from his commitment. And in so doing, Dr. King changed the nation forever.

NOTES

1. Jonathan Weisman, "In Their Own Words: Staff Sgt. Chris Bain," *The Washington Post*, March 19, 2006.
2. Ibid.
3. Ibid.
4. Clayborne Carson, ed., *The Autobiography of Martin Luther King, Jr.* (New York: Warner Books, 1998), 15.
5. Ibid., 137, 138–39.
6. Ibid., 153–54.
7. Ibid., 155.
8. C.S. Lewis, *Chronicles of Narnia: The Silver Chair* (New York: HarperCollins, 2001), 557–58.

Chapter VI

THE LEVERAGE

The origin of the lever as a tool to multiply force dates back far beyond antiquity; its workings were first described by the greatest mathematician in the ancient world Archimedes in the third century BC. A lever (usually a long, rigid object such as a board) uses a relatively small amount of applied force to lift or move a much heavier object.

Leverage works through the phenomenon of balance, the same phenomenon that produces the up and down motion of a child's teeter-totter. Place a heavy weight on one end of the lever, a lighter weight on the opposite end. Set a fulcrum, or pivot point, under the lever between the middle of the lever and the heavier weight. Then push down on the opposite end of the lever, and the heavier weight is raised. The position of the fulcrum determines the degree of leverage that can be achieved. At some point along the length of the lever, the two weights will balance each other, like two children on the teeter-totter. As we move the fulcrum toward the heavier weight, the amount of leverage increases until a

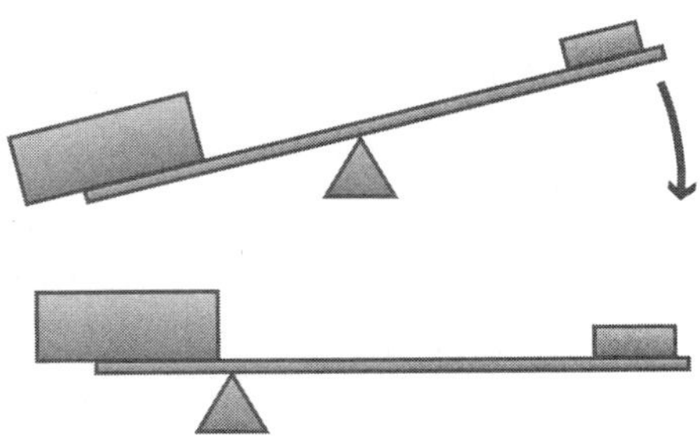

very light application of weight on the far end of the lever can easily lift or move the heavier weight.

INFLUENCE—THE "SOME CONTROL" CHOICE

The principle of leverage provides a good metaphor when we run into a situation where we might have a degree of control in finding ways around a barrier or a major obstacle in our path. In a world full of no control, some control, and total control situations, we need to recognize that the most common of these conditions is *some* control. In reality, *all* situations involving other people are situations where we only have, at best, some control.

If you stop to think about it, you will notice numerous situations in life where "some control" is the best description of your degree of control. In chapter 4, we noted that in a "some control" situation, the opposites on the spectrum of responses were *influence* and *manipulate.* And if the leverage of influence produces far more productive and positive approaches to dealing with others than manipulation, influence becomes not only a necessary lever in confronting challenging times, but also a skill that can be applied to all relationships and situations.

In an increasingly confrontational society, we seem to forget the need for a more productive and positive approach to influencing situations and solving problems. I strongly believe that effective solutions are best achieved through mutual respect and mutual effort. I also believe the following statements are true and foundational for anyone seeking to have a quality life in the world today:

- The quality of our life is a function of the quality of our relationships.
- Relationships that endure and prosper require mutual benefit.
- The quality of our relationships is a function of how well we communicate.
- We want quality, lasting, mutually satisfying relationships.

Aristotle taught that we are rational beings, with the rational aspect of the soul divided into two contrasting parts—an intellectual part and an emotional part. Roderick T. Long, a professor of philosophy at Auburn University, spoke about these two parts of our rational selves in a post-9/11 address: "Both parts are rational; and both parts are needed to give us proper sensitivity to the moral nuances of the situations that confront us"[1] Nothing is more difficult than managing a challenging situation in which emotion is at a maximum and is suppressing normally rational responses and consideration. The best antidote I know for these types of highly charged and emotional situations is to practice influence.

Note that there are limits to influence, to negotiation, and to patience. Years ago, I found an interesting and inspiring exploration of these limits in the seminal work on families and relationships done by the Colorado-based author and parenting lecturer Barbara Coloroso.

She describes three kinds of families, based on three methods of parenting. In the "Jellyfish" (permissive) family, anything goes. For the "Brick Wall" (authoritarian) family, there is a rule for everything. Her third category, the "Backbone" (in the middle) family, works best because it mixes flexibility with setting limits. Coloroso explains:

> A Backbone family says to kids, mistakes are okay. Mistakes are for learning. A Backbone family also invites kids at a very young age to make responsible choices, and when they make unwise choices, they (the parents) stick with them and say, 'Kid, you can fix this'. They say, 'Kid you have a problem; I know you can handle it.' And in the end the child knows how to think, not just what to think. And within himself, he's developing a backbone for his own moral sense of what's right, what's wrong.[2]

From her work, I have developed the following simple rule:

Bend on process. Stand on principle. Know the difference.

And, also based on Barbara Coloroso's work, the issues of principle include safety, morality, and legality.

TO PIERCE OR NOT TO PIERCE

When my daughter was fourteen years old, she came to me with a declaration posing as a conversation. "Dad," she said, "I want to pierce my eyebrow, and I want to pierce my navel." For me, in this moment, the fantasy of fatherhood fully and immediately confronted the real world.

Because I had been teaching the concept of leverage and influence to others, I felt I should apply it myself. Our conversation went something like this:

"Rachel, do you want a part-time job while you are in high school?" Yes, she hoped that would happen.

"Do you want to get into a specific university once you graduate from high school and get a scholarship?" Yes, that would be desirable as well.

"Then," I said, "You cannot pierce your eyebrow."

"Why not?"

"Well," I said, "because old people like me run the world." She looked at me both puzzled and frustrated. I continued, "Old people like me are generally—not always, but generally—more conservative than younger people. And," I said, "we don't like facial piercings."

"That's not fair," she retorted.

My response: "I know, but we're not talking fair, we're talking real."

"I still don't get your point," she replied.

"Well," I said, "it may not be fair, but it's a fact that older people control who gets the jobs, who gets the admissions, and who gets the scholarships." I tried to help her understand that most of her desired outcomes would require face-to-face interviews and that facial piercings could have a negative impact on her chances.

In this conversation, which started with me trying to talk sense into my daughter, the failure of influence caused me to ask a principle/process question and decide (based on her goals, not mine) whether or not this was a place where I needed to take a stand—to take total control and act.

"What about my navel?" she then asked. Well, I decided, in for a penny—in for a pound. In my own mind, my mental conversation went like this:

Is piercing your navel, if done properly, unsafe? . . . No.

Is piercing your navel, with parental consent, illegal? (In our jurisdiction, the law required parental consent for piercing or tattooing under the age of eighteen.) . . . No.

Is piercing your navel, immoral? My values, which I hoped I shared with her, argued for "yes," but it was not a definitive yes at that time. And since in my fantasy world of fatherhood, no one except her husband in a far distant future would ever see it and the piercing could largely remain hidden, I knew in my mind what my answer needed to be. Having failed my own imposed test for influence—no unsafe, illegal, or immoral consequences—character required me to say, "You can pierce your navel."

Now, you may think I am totally off base in this decision. Your acceptance of the approach, your use of the tool and the outcomes, may be very different. But I believe this mental approach has practical value, especially when dealing with difficult situations. And using this approach allows you to preserve the power and leverage of influence without being held eternally captive to situations where influence is obviously stalemated, if not stone-cold dead.

When I teach the principle of influence in my seminars, I like to pose the following questions to the group:

- Does influence always work? . . . No.
- What do you do if influence fails to move the situation forward?

I think the answer to the second question lies in the summary above. If the situation needing resolution is one of principle, where the safety, morality, or legality for all those involved would be impacted negatively, then we must move to a position of total control and act. Find a way to take appropriate control.

INFLUENCE IN A WAR OR PEACE SITUATION

The careful use of influence can also be applied to situations that have national or worldwide implications. The event known as the Cuban Missile Crisis provides a classic example of using the leverage of influence to disarm a potentially disastrous situation. In October 1962, events initiated by Nikita Khrushchev, the impetuous and unpredictable leader of the Soviet Union, triggered the crisis. He believed at the time—rightly or wrongly—that the United States had far more intercontinental ballistic missiles than the Russian military had. In what historian Paul Johnson, in *A History of the American People,* called "an absurdly dangerous move," Khrushchev persuaded Cuban leader Fidel Castro to allow the Soviet Union to station medium-range missiles in Cuba, less than one hundred miles from the United States mainland. The Cuban dictator later told French newspaper reporters, "The initial idea originated with the Russians and with them alone. . . . It was not in order to insure our defense but primarily to strengthen socialism on the international plane."[3]

As the Russians began to move support troops and missiles into Cuba, American intelligence services took notice and began flying regular high-altitude U-2 reconnaissance missions to monitor the situation. The Soviet leader sent assurances to the President that only surface-to-air missiles and support troops were being sent to Cuba, for purely "defensive" purposes. But on October 16, Khrushchev's "promises" were revealed as untrue. That day intelligence officials showed President John F. Kennedy and several key advisors evidence from detailed reconnaissance photos that sites in Cuba were being prepared for missile launchers. Stockpiles of what appeared to be nuclear-armed, medium-range missiles were already on the ground. Intelligence experts estimated that by December, about fifty strategic missiles would be deployed, capable of destroying America's main defense systems in seventeen minutes.

Robert F. "Bobby" Kennedy, the President's younger brother and attorney general, attended the meeting and played a key role in the crisis, both before and after the photographs revealed the presence of Soviet missiles. A few weeks prior to the arrival of this intelligence, the younger Kennedy had met with Soviet Ambassador Anatoly Dobrynin, with whom the attorney general had developed a personal relationship. This relationship and the opportunities for influence it provided turned out to be one of several leveraging factors in the eventual outcome of what was emerging as a very dangerous situation.

"I told Ambassador Dobrynin of President Kennedy's deep concern about what was happening [in the shipments to Cuba]," Robert Kennedy later wrote in *Thirteen Days*, his account of the crisis. "He told me I should not be concerned, for he was instructed by Soviet Chairman Nikita S. Khrushchev to assure President Kennedy that there would be no ground-to-ground missiles or offensive weapons placed in Cuba."[4] About this same time, the Soviet embassy delivered a personal message from the Russian leader to the president, giving assurance that "under no circumstances would surface-to-surface missiles be sent to Cuba."[5]

With the most recent aerial photographs clearly showing Khrushchev to be lying, President Kennedy and his advisors turned to a discussion of appropriate responses for the United States to take. They formed a special task force, "Ex Comm," to determine a response and coordinate the efforts of the nation's defense, intelligence, and diplomatic efforts. It soon became evident that the participants were divided into several different camps. One faction, including most of the military leadership, advocated immediate military action to destroy the missiles and launch sites and, if necessary, invade Cuba to settle the long-festering relationship with Castro once and for all.

Another group argued against military strikes because of the possibility of accidentally triggering a nuclear conflict. They instead favored direct and "under the radar" diplomacy to find a peaceful solution that would remove the missiles and allow both the United States and the Soviet Union to save face.

Still others felt that America should offer to remove some of its own missiles aimed at the Russians and to placate the Soviet Union in other ways. In Robert Kennedy's words, "And so we argued, and so we disagreed—all dedicated, intelligent men, disagreeing and fighting about the future of their country, and of mankind. Meanwhile, time was running out."[6]

After much deliberation among the group, President Kennedy took a middle ground approach, directing the US Navy to establish a "quarantine," or blockade, on maritime shipping to Cuba, with orders to turn away or seize any ships carrying weapons. The President did have total control of this one aspect of the situation, and he exercised his ability to act.

The blockade was intended to show the ability of the United States to use its power to protect its interests. In spite of the risk that one mistakenly fired shot or torpedo could trigger a full-fledged naval battle, President Kennedy implemented this solution in part to provide an environment that would buy enough time for influence to work. As Bobby Kennedy wrote, his feeling was "that [the blockade] had more flexibilities and fewer liabilities than a military attack."[7] The President, remembering the chain of missteps that had ultimately started World War I in 1914, said to the group upon announcing his decision, "The great danger and risk in all of this is a miscalculation—a mistake in judgment."[8]

With the blockade in place, the next step in this delicate dance needed to come from the Soviet Union. Would they choose to defy the blockade and initiate military action? Or would they see that further pursuit of their now-revealed missile plan was not worth continuing? At the same time, full-scale efforts to leverage a favorable decision were initiated through direct diplomacy with allies as well as discussions through backwater diplomatic channels. The US State Department initiated a special meeting of the Organization of American States and was successful in obtaining the unanimous support of Latin American nations for the removal of the Russian missiles. Ideas quietly circulated suggesting the possibility of the United States removing obsolete intercontinental missiles stationed in Turkey, directly across the Black Sea from the Soviet Union. The President also sent a direct message to Khrushchev clearly stating that the United States did not want to fire on Soviet ships that might defy the blockade, and urging the Russian leader to observe the quarantine.

To unite world opinion, the United States also took its case to the United Nations. Coming into that meeting, the Soviet Union's position was that the missiles were purely defensive, and several European countries expressed doubts about the evidence of missiles in Cuba. In the United Nations Security Council, America's UN Ambassador, Adlai Stevenson, had a dramatic confrontation with the Soviet UN delegate. Stevenson asked the Soviet delegate point-blank if he denied that the Soviet Union had placed or was placing intermediate-range missiles at sites in Cuba. The Soviet delegate shot back an angry reply, "I am not in an American courtroom!" and refused to answer Stevenson's question. At that point, the US Ambassador revealed the latest photographs of the Cuban sites, clearly showing Russian offensive missiles. The photographs had, as Robert Kennedy put it, "devastating effect."[9] In the hours and days to follow, the majority of world opinion moved clearly behind the United States.

Tensions continued to rise during the next few days as the navy stopped and boarded several ships, but no shots were fired. On October 25, President Kennedy contacted Khrushchev, again asking that he remove the missiles. Two days later, he received a personally written letter from Nikita Khrushchev. In it, the Soviet leader proposed to stop further weapons shipments to Cuba and to withdraw or destroy those already there "if assurances were given that the President of the United States would not participate in an attack on Cuba and the blockade [was] lifted." He then used the analogy of the two nations each pulling "on the ends of the rope in which you have tied the knot of war, because the more the two of us pull, the tighter the knot will be tied. . . . Then let us not only relax the forces pulling on the ends of the rope, let us take measures to untie that knot. We are ready for this."[10]

Influence had worked in this potentially catastrophic situation, averting the potential for a nuclear holocaust. Although leaders involved in the negotiations experienced a few rough spots in the following days, the crisis was essentially over. The Russians removed the missiles, the United States lifted the blockade, and although it was not part of the original agreement, President Kennedy later quietly removed the American missiles in Turkey as a show of good faith. The world breathed a collective sigh of relief as events and decisions that could have escalated into a catastrophe were averted.

Daunting and pivotal challenges have arisen throughout our nation's history, and we can expect them to appear in the future. I believe that our best chance for engaging appropriately with a challenging and complex world lies in knowing when to influence, when to adapt, and when to act. In most instances, influence can be a valuable tool in finding and implementing good solutions. In other situations, such as a future attack on our territory or vital interests, we as individuals and as a nation will need to stand up and, if necessary, move to total control and act accordingly. But in so doing, we should act only when we are certain that our choices are well thought out and informed—considered not by expediency alone, but by thoughtful review of process and principle.

Seeking to influence is a critical first step in dealing with the difficult situations that occur between people or groups of people. But an individual or group also needs to recognize when influence will not affect a situation or when it no longer works. They must also identify subsequent steps that will channel energy toward positive and productive results.

John F. Kennedy did not talk America's way out of the Cuban Missile Crisis. He used the lever of influence overtly and covertly, he knew when and where to adapt and when to let things go, and he knew when it was time to act—to draw a line in the Caribbean Sea and challenge the Soviets to stand down. Many of his advisors argued for unilateral and inflexible approaches. Some advocated simply accepting and adapting, while others advised early and aggressive action, and still others were for exercising patience and unending influence. The successful outcome of this seminal moment in history bears witness of the benefits of a careful and mature response. It was not the result of John Kennedy's or Bobby Kennedy's or anyone's actions alone, but it was the outcome of having a careful and mature hand on the tiller.

THE LEVERAGE: Key Principles to Remember

President John F. Kennedy taught us . . .

BY CREATING TRUST WE CREATE A LEVEL OF COMMITMENT THAT BRINGS OTHERS TOGETHER TO ACHIEVE A GREAT GOAL

- A physical lever, used to move or lift large items, is a force multiplier. It takes the energy of one person and makes it equal to the force of many.
- President Kennedy, like all of us, was not perfect. But he was sufficiently trustworthy to hold his team and our nation together and bring us through one of the most terrifying periods of America's history.
- People follow others they trust. By working to become more personally trustworthy we will find it easier to obtain and maintain the help and support of others in worthy causes that affect us all.

NOTES

1. Roderick T. Long, address on October 5, 2001.
2. Barbara Coloroso, http://www.kidsareworthit.com.
3. Paul Johnson, *A History of the American People* (New York: HarperCollins, 1998), 862.
4. Robert F. Kennedy, *Thirteen Days: A Memoir of the Cuban Missile Crisis* (New York: W.W. Norton, 1971), 21.
5. Ibid., 22.
6. Ibid., 28.
7. Ibid., 29.
8. Ibid., 49.
9 Ibid., 59.
10. Ibid., 61.

Chapter VII

THE LEADER

In challenging times, we find moments and situations when each of us must become leaders in our own spheres of influence. In some situations, adapting or influencing can be either impossible or counterproductive. At times we may need to act in opposition to prevailing opinion or predominating information. Never act rashly or without deeply considering the challenge and its possible solutions and consequences. But remember the difference between consideration and procrastination; it's easy and tempting to replace consideration with procrastination.

ACT RATHER THAN PROCRASTINATE

Early in our marriage, Heather and I were window-shopping in a mall. We came upon a jewelry shop that was going out of business and advertising up to 90 percent off everything in the store. We stopped at the display windows to see what remained on offer. There, on prominent display, was a large cushion-cut emerald ring. Now, Heather loved emeralds and had spoken to me of that love many times in the past. The ring was truly on sale for a very reasonable price but, as Heather explained, we were poor students. Knowing how much she wanted it, I argued we could find a way to afford it, and at its reduced price, purchasing the ring was not totally out of the realm of possibility. But Heather, exercising her inborn caution, thought we should think about it and maybe return the next day. Rather than buy the ring then and there, we chose procrastination. Well, we did return the next day and—you know what happened—the ring was gone.

Now, every time either of us thinks the other is unnecessarily or unreasonably procrastinating when action is demanded, we just say, "Remember the emerald ring."

WHEN ACTING CAN HAVE GLOBAL IMPLICATIONS

I realize the great difference in both scope and impact between buying jewelry and leading a country and the world away from the precipice of nuclear annihilation. But the same choices lie at their roots—to act or to procrastinate.

In general, the American electorate believes strongly that leaders—especially government leaders—should understand what the majority wants and then follow those wishes. The best leaders understand that they should listen to and take counsel from those they lead or represent, but at times they must also act and make decisions that may be in opposition to the popular sentiments of the time or even to the advice of colleagues, counselors, and "experts."

Ronald Reagan presents one of the best examples of an American President acting—boldly, firmly, and against the counsel of many of his key advisors. Action, which he consistently applied to the relationship between the Soviet Union and the United States, eventually caused a shift in the power struggle, creating one of the most significant changes in world relations in the last century.

Some historians consider the late 1970s and early 1980s to be the zenith of what we have come to call the Cold War, the forty-five-year-long nuclear standoff between the United States, along with the other Western Democracies, and the Communist-ruled Union of Soviet

Socialist Republics, the collective name of the combination of Russia and other nations long occupied by Russia.

In the final years of the Carter presidency, many at home and abroad perceived the United States to be faltering in economic growth and prosperity, and falling behind in confronting the growing military threat represented by the Soviet Union. As the oil-producing states of the Middle East grouped together in the OPEC cartel, raising and lowering petroleum prices and output at will, gasoline shortages and skyrocketing prices gave many Americans a feeling of helplessness.

This feeling of helplessness increased with a revolution in Iran in 1979 that brought an extremist and militant Islamist government into power. The new Iranian leadership was violently anti-American, resulting in the subsequent storming of the American embassy by "students," who held 109 members of the embassy staff hostage for more than a year. An attempted American military operation to free the hostages ended tragically, aborted at a midway gathering point when a helicopter collided with a transport aircraft, killing eight men and destroying several other aircraft. To some at home and many abroad, the United States seemed to be declining as the government floundered in the foreign affairs arena.

At the same time, the Soviet Union appeared to be building its military strength. Intelligence sources indicated that the Soviets had achieved a sizable advantage in nuclear-armed ICBMs (intercontinental ballistic missiles). With the Soviet Union emboldened by the perception of a faltering America, diplomatic relations between the two adversaries seemed to be approaching a new peak of hostility and suspicion about each other's motives. Wars of words flew back and forth, sabers rattled, and pompous threats and denunciations issued from both sides.

The outcome of the Presidential election of 1980 rested on the perception that Ronald Reagan was more willing to stand up to the Soviet

Union, as well as his call for a return to the days of America's greatness as a world leader. In Reagan's first Presidential news conference, a reporter asked a question about détente, a then-popular idea aimed at finding a way to come to some kind of "accommodation" with the Soviets that would make both sides happy. To the dismay of Al Haig, his newly sworn-in secretary of state, President Reagan didn't mince any words. After noting his view that détente had "been a one-way street that the Soviet Union has used to pursue its own aims," Reagan went on to say, as reported by historian Michael Beschloss in his book *Presidential Courage*,

> The Soviets sought a "one-world Communist state," reserving for themselves "the right to commit any crime, to lie, to cheat."
>
> After the President spoke, there was "an audible gasp" in the room. Standing by a wall Al Haig rolled his eyes at Reagan's undiplomatic language. No president since at least Kennedy had talked so tough about the Kremlin in public.[1]

This statement by the new President drew an angry response from Soviet leaders, but it put the world on notice that this chief executive was different than his immediate predecessors.

Later that spring, Reagan was the target of an unsuccessful assassination attempt, in which he was seriously wounded. During his recovery, he had much time to think, and he came to feel that his life had been spared in order to lessen the risk of nuclear war.

Forsaking some of the hawkish tone in his earlier statements about the Soviet Union—including calling the Soviet Union an "evil empire"—he decided to write a personal letter to Leonid Brezhnev, the Communist party general secretary and Soviet dictator, to communicate his desire for, in his words, "a world without nuclear weapons." Despite attempts by Secretary Haig to change the wording to be more "diplomatic," Reagan prevailed, and the final message still reflected much of his feelings and emotions about this issue.

Brezhnev responded in a somewhat mocking manner, but the President's letter formed the beginning of a personal dialogue between the determined Reagan and the hard-line Brezhnev as well as his revolving-door successors in the Kremlin over the next few years. Neither side seemed willing to give an inch, but over time, the correspondence resulted in a greater degree of mutual discussion about nuclear weapons reductions and other issues that divided the two superpowers.

President Reagan also had to do battle on these issues with several groups in his administration. The diplomatic establishment and some members of the National Security Council pushed for a harder line with the Soviets, with no reductions in armaments. The President recorded in his diary that these advisors "don't think any approach should be made to the Soviets. I think I'm hard line and will never appease. But I do want to try to let them see there is a better world if they'll show *by deed* they want to get along with the Free World."[2]

Reagan stood by his mission. In time, he announced (with little consultation from those he knew would oppose) that the United States would develop a Strategic Defense Initiative (SDI) that would provide a defensive shield against missiles from the Soviet Union or anywhere else, for that matter. His critics "derided SDI as 'Star Wars'—a harebrained scheme that would cost too much and never work."[3] This initiative alarmed the Soviet leadership because they felt they could not match American technology and they feared that this advantage would allow the United States to unilaterally attack and conquer the Soviet Union.

At times during this period, relations became especially tense between the two adversaries, most notably in 1983 when, for unfathomable reasons, Soviet fighter jets shot down Korean Air Lines flight 007 over the north Pacific. The Soviets claimed the airliner was an American spy plane, and the incident cost the lives of 269 innocent people.

Reagan denounced the attack as the "Korean Air Line massacre," and relations were frosty for a time.

In a January 1984 speech from the White House, Reagan said that the Soviet Union could no longer "underestimate our strength or question our resolve." But rather than lambasting the Soviets as an "evil empire" as he had in the past, the President sought to find new ways to create "a constructive working relationship," one that could allow both sides to reduce their nuclear arsenals.

In March of 1985, a new Soviet leader, Mikhail Gorbachev, emerged as the latest in a line of briefly appointed leaders of the Soviet Union, each of whom had died or left office after a short tenure. As time would prove, Gorbachev would turn out to be a completely new kind of Soviet leader—pragmatic, realistically aware of his country's strengths and weaknesses, and willing to take a fresh look at ways to end decades of distrust and animosity between the Soviet Union and the United States.

Determined to continue his efforts toward achieving mutually agreeable nuclear arms reductions, President Reagan persisted in his quest, eager to get to know this new Soviet leader and develop a working relationship with him. And by this time, he had a majority of the American people and most of the formerly skeptical members of his administration behind his efforts. Despite some rocky bumps and jolts in the beginning, the two leaders came to have great mutual respect and admiration, and eventually forged a trust and friendship that would change the world dynamic that had existed since the end of World War II.

At their first meeting, in a villa near Geneva, Switzerland, they did not resolve any of the differences that stood between them, but they established a less formal approach to their discussions. Despite concerns by both nations' diplomats that they were not being "diplomatic," they seemed to approach the occasion as two individuals speaking frankly and honestly with each other. Soon the American President and the Soviet Communist General Secretary were exchanging jokes and making friendly gibes with each other. They talked about SDI; the Soviet leader obviously feared the possible strategic imbalance that would result from America's successful completion of a missile defense system. Reagan surprised the Soviet leader by offering to share American antimissile research with the Soviets, something that Gorbachev thought would never really happen. They left with an agreement to remain in contact with each other and to meet again over the next two years.

Reagan and Gorbachev met for the second time in October 1986 in Reykjavik, Iceland, a neutral location where both felt that they could meet privately without a lot of attention from hundreds of journalists or a host government that might want to be a part of the action. At this "mini-summit," they continued to refine their thinking about nuclear arms reductions and the Soviet concerns about the Strategic Defense Initiative. On arms reduction, Reagan kept repeating the mantra, "Trust, but verify," to the point where it became a joke. In subsequent discussions, Gorbachev would dramatically clap his hands over his ears at the mention of the phrase. But because of the familiar relationship they formed, Gorbachev offered to help his colleagues overcome long-held aversion to any kind of on-site inspections. And once again, Reagan offered to share the missile shield technology with the Soviets, but Gorbachev said he still could not take the idea seriously and preferred that the Americans would simply drop the program.

Despite disagreements on some issues, the two still emerged from the Reykjavik meetings as friends, with a desire to continue the discussions and try to implement the kinds of mutual changes they had discussed. Although they came, in Reagan's words, "this close" (picture a thumb and forefinger almost touching) to a nuclear agreement that would have eventually done away with all American and Soviet nuclear arms, the SDI issue was a sore point to the end, and the meetings ended with an unspoken agreement to disagree on that and to hold off on the more drastic nuclear reduction options.

SDI proved to be a strong motivation for the Soviets to eventually come to some kind of agreement. Reagan came away with the impression that the Soviets couldn't possibly spend the kind of money the United States was spending on developing SDI. If the Soviets tried to keep up, it would, in Reagan's terms, "break" them—a supposition proved true after the breakup of the Soviet Union.

In June 1987, the American President visited Berlin and gave a speech at the Brandenburg Gate, then part of the infamous Berlin Wall erected by Russian troops in 1961 to keep East Germans from escaping to West Germany. Angered by the sight of East Germans being herded away from the area by the guards, an angry Reagan shouted, loudly enough for those on the other side of the wall to hear:

> General Secretary Gorbachev, if you seek peace, if you seek prosperity for the Soviet Union and Eastern Europe, if you seek liberalization: Come here to this gate! Mr. Gorbachev, open this gate! Mr. Gorbachev, tear down this wall!

Although that admonition was not immediately heeded, in 1989 Mikhail Gorbachev did open the gate, and the wall came down during the final stages of the dissolution of the Soviet Empire, ending the division of Europe that had occurred in the aftermath of World War II.

As a final footnote to the success of Ronald Reagan's dogged determination to change the dynamic of the Cold War, the two leaders met in Washington, DC, on December 8, 1987, to sign the Intermediate-Range Nuclear Forces (INF) Treaty, the first step toward the larger nuclear reductions both leaders had discussed at their earlier meetings and in their official correspondence between meetings.

In May of 1992, Gorbachev visited the retired American President at his Santa Barbara ranch, Rancho del Cielo. They rode around the ranch in Reagan's blue Jeep and relived some of the events that they had shared over the years. As a final quip after being told about all the fences that Reagan had personally built at the ranch, Gorbachev reprised Reagan's oft repeated phrase in the negotiations, "Trust, but verify," and the two former adversaries laughed.

Michael Beschloss provides perhaps the best summary of how these unlikely results came from what started out as an extremely confrontational relationship between an American President and his Soviet counterparts:

> Unlike more ordinary politicians who followed the slightest downdraft in the political atmosphere, Ronald Reagan's strong beliefs and optimism moved him to do things from which others might have flinched. . . .
>
> Although more than willing to adjust his rhetoric, Reagan felt that if his anti-Soviet belligerence scared [Americans], they were welcome to vote against him. As promised, he used his landslide victory as a mandate to set about convincing the Russians that America had regained its political will. . . .
>
> Reagan had always told the public that if turning up the pressure on the Soviets made them bargain seriously, he would not only deal but try to abolish nuclear weapons. When they heard this, many of his conservative champions had winked, presuming that he really didn't believe it.
>
> But when Gorbachev showed that he had similar ambitions, Reagan proved that he meant what he said. At Reykjavik, he tried to end the nuclear arms race once and for all—even if it infuriated some of his earliest supporters. Like most effective American Presidents, Reagan ultimately proved that he was not the captive of his political base, but its leader.[4]

In challenging times and in situations where you do have total or near-total control, use caution, practice restraint, check and recheck, but above all, follow your deeply held convictions in the matter, acting on your chosen course. And at the same time, keep in mind Reagan's approach to "trust, but verify."

There is much to be learned from someone like Ronald Reagan, who had the courage of his convictions. Of course, Reagan was a human being and, like all of us, his motives were not always perfectly pure or his behavior totally noble. But many Americans, when asked to list the greatest of American presidents, are increasingly including Ronald Reagan in a short but lofty list that almost always includes Franklin Delano Roosevelt, George Washington, Thomas Jefferson, and Abraham Lincoln. And I think that those presidents make that list because of their defining decisions—decisions made out of a determination to bring about significant changes in long-standing ways of doing the nation's business. When we (or a president or any leader) are confronted with decisions, the easy choice may be to procrastinate or decide in favor of political or popular outcomes, but the ability to act—based upon fact, conviction, and trust—may be essential to literally saving the world.

THE LEADER: Key Principles to Remember

President Ronald Reagan taught us . . .

GOOD SOLUTIONS MAY REQUIRE US TO USE A VARIETY OF DECISION MAKING APPROACHES, APPROPRIATE TO THE SITUATION WE ARE CONFRONTING

- Most people and, in fact, most leaders tend to become obsessed with a single way to decide, and they use that approach even when it doesn't make sense. President Reagan's skill with multiple decision-making approaches and his personal flexibility in their use allowed a difficult and time-consuming situation to come to a solution far sooner and far better than anyone could imagine.

NOTES

1. Michael Beschloss, *Presidential Courage: Brave Leaders and How They Changed America* (New York: Simon & Schuster, 2007), 283.
2. Ibid., 291.
3. Ibid., 293.
4. Ibid., 323–24.

Chapter VIII

THE LIBERATION

Considering the larger human experience, especially in times of challenge, can help people better recognize a common reality. As we have looked to the great leaders discussed in this book, we have witnessed the power of adapting, influencing, or acting in difficult or challenging situations. Individually or collectively, making these kinds of choices has not necessarily meant that they were the "right" or "best" or "only" choices for meeting the challenges they faced. In some cases, the choices these leaders made were not necessarily popular or acceptable to all. But overall, their choices moved us forward as a nation and as individuals.

Because we encounter national challenges as separate groups and as individuals as well as a nation, we will always find differing opinions about the nature of the danger, the approach to meeting it, and the best possible outcome. Sometimes these differences can be managed, with relationships preserved and emotions soothed. At other times, because of the nature of the challenge and the possible outcomes, the results may not please or satisfy all those affected.

No one can bring back the child killed in an unfortunate encounter with a drunk driver, or reverse the consequences of war. Even when drastic differences between groups or individuals can be bridged or resolved to the satisfaction of most involved, lingering hurt and feelings of betrayal may remain. At these times where gaps remain and results are unalterable, simply adapting, influencing, or acting may not be enough to make everything "all better." Relationships—whether between countries, cultures, groups, or individuals—cannot always be returned to what they were before the challenge.

In such moments, it is too easy to be angry and to be torn apart when, in fact, the very thing that is needed is to come together—as did Washington and his troops at Valley Forge or John F. Kennedy and his cabinet in the midst of the Cuban Missile Crisis. Remembering the human connection helps to replace cynicism with synergy, and bluster with brotherhood.

THE FORGIVENESS OPTION

In your own struggles, when confronted with obstacles that have left you wearied, feeling estranged from others, and frustrated at your current plight, the best solution may lie in your efforts to unite with those around you instead of the natural urge to separate from those who have wronged you. In such situations, setting aside the wrong and forgiving others may be the only way to achieve the resolution and inner peace you desire.

James E. Faust, a leader in my community, gave a powerful speech several years ago in which he addressed the need for greater public understanding and forgiveness in the face of seemingly unconquerable challenges and tragedy. He spoke of the impact and example of a friend and community leader whose son, a lawyer, had been killed by a bomb intentionally planted by a client who was trying to cover up his own criminal activity. This violent deed had not only left a wife and young family without their father, but also traumatized the slain man's extended family. With the news media hounding the extended family for their reaction, the father of the man who was killed realized, "This thing will destroy my family if we don't forgive. Venom and hatred will never end if we do not put this out of our system."

In relating this family's experience, Faust said, "Healing and peace came as the family cleansed their hearts from anger and were able to forgive the man who took their son's life." He also said,

> All of us suffer some injuries from experiences that seem to have no rhyme or reason. We cannot understand them. We may never know why some things happen in this life. . . . But because it happens, it must be endured. . . . If we can find forgiveness in our hearts for those who have caused us hurt and injury, we will rise to a higher level of self-esteem and wellbeing. Some recent studies show that people who are taught to forgive become 'less angry, more hopeful, less depressed, less anxious and less stressed,' which leads to greater physical wellbeing. Another of these studies concludes 'that forgiveness . . . is a liberating gift [that] people can give to themselves.'[1]

Remember the "lion in the way" metaphor used in chapter 5? You may not have to deal with a lion that is as tragic and overwhelming as having a loved one murdered. But you will likely find yourself dealing with life challenges that seem to defy solution. In such instances, what happened may be a no control situation, but you do have some control over how you react and what you do. Since these difficult situations often involve your relationships with other people, remember the forgiveness option before you find yourself trapped in loathing and self-pity, consumed by anger.

A friend of mine who is involved in family therapy and counseling recounted to me a frustrating attempt to bring together two grown siblings, a man and a woman, who had let childhood rivalries and disagreements fester into a decades-long estrangement. Their lives seemed to be consumed in jealousy and blame, and it affected the relationships in their extended family. My friend, the counselor for one of these individuals, had been in contact with a similar counselor working with the other. The therapists set up a meeting between the two combatants with the hope of finding some way to help them reconcile.

While things started out amiably, sparks and accusations soon started to fly, with the two siblings going at each other about who was to blame for this offense or that slight over the years. They had etched the patterns of blame and mutual hatred so deeply onto their Belief Windows that erasing them seemed impossible. After more than an hour of dispute, the meeting was adjourned and both adversaries left in a huff. The two counselors shook their heads in dismay and wonder at how patterns so ingrained had come to dominate and consume the lives of these two otherwise good people.

FROM ENEMIES TO ALLIES

Just as forgiveness offers a path to more cohesive relationships on an individual level, approaching the difficult situations facing groups or nations with an attitude of forgiveness can create a path toward unification rather than isolation. The events surrounding the February 1945 battle on the barren volcanic island of Iwo Jima demonstrate the healing and peace that forgiveness offers individuals and groups.

The final year of the Second World War had turned out to be the most difficult year for both the Americans and the Japanese, and the battle at Iwo Jima was one of the costliest in terms of lives lost. In the words of historian Stephen Ambrose, the combat at Iwo Jima "was waged with a barbarism and race hatred staggering in scope, savage almost beyond belief, and catastrophic in consequence. Each side regarded the other as subhuman vermin." In more than three years of bloody encounters, both sides had come to hate their enemy to the point that the conflict had become, as Ambrose called it, "a war without mercy."[2]

Iwo Jima lay only eight hundred miles from the Japanese home islands, and with three airfields, it was needed by the United States as a staging base for the planned assault on the Japanese home islands. The Japanese viewed Iwo Jima as a final point of defense for their sacred homeland, to be held to the last man. The Japanese had committed 22,000 troops to Iwo Jima's defense and had laid minefields and constructed a honeycomb of tunnels and bunkers throughout the island.

After bombardment from American battleships and cruisers, the invasion of Iwo Jima began on the morning of February 19, 1945. Once ashore, the US Marines ran into difficulty moving themselves and their equipment through the volcanic ash and sand that covered much of the island, including the beaches. The Japanese defenders had been ordered to hold fire until the beaches were full of American marines and their equipment. Then from their hidden locations, they opened fire on the struggling marines, and the battle began in earnest. In Ambrose's words,

> The marines took Iwo by crawling forward on their stomachs or behind tanks that bogged down in the volcanic ash. Men with rifles and flamethrowers fought their way from pillbox to foxhole, climbing the dominant defensive feature, rocky Mount Surabachi, where on February 23, after three days of furious combat, the marines hoisted the Stars and Stripes and photographer Joe Rosenthal of the Associated Press took one of the war's most famous pictures.[3]

What the Americans had expected to be a three- or four-day operation dragged on into weeks of mopping up, cleaning out all of the underground strongholds, and securing the island. Both sides fought unrelentingly; but the battle-hardened Americans finally subdued the Japanese defenders, who had been ordered to fight to the death. When combat ceased after a month of fierce fighting, only a few hundred of the 22,000 Japanese defenders survived. Of the 100,000 Americans who stormed ashore, the death toll was 6,825 killed in action, with more than 20,000 wounded.

Separated from those bloody days by more than a half century, many Americans today have difficulty comprehending the ferocity and anger on both sides of the battle of Iwo Jima. In 1985, the fortieth anniversary of the landing by the American marines, a commemorative event called the "Reunion of Honor" was held on this isolated and tiny island. Planners of the event hoped that survivors from both sides would be able to come together and feel some degree of reconciliation.

Could any of them ever forget what had happened there? My coauthor Hyrum Smith has talked with several marine veterans who fought at Iwo Jima; they affirmed that they "will never forget." Hyrum tells of his experience a few years ago watching a documentary about Iwo Jima and what he assumed was that first reunion of the battle's veterans in 1985. Many of the surviving marines who received invitations to this "reunion" with their enemies declined to go. Why go and bring back all of the horror and nightmare memories of that experience? For these veterans, there was no way they could ever forgive these people for what they had undergone at Iwo Jima. No doubt some of the Japanese survivors felt the same way. But in the end, several hundred of these former marines attended the reunion, and over one hundred of the former Japanese soldiers accepted the invitation.

The documentary showed two groups of men arriving on the island. The former marines stood on one side of the airstrip; the Japanese veterans on the other. For some time they just stood there and looked nervously at each other. Then without warning, a spontaneous outburst of love and forgiveness exploded over the runway. The two groups of men literally ran across the airstrip and threw their arms around each other as they wept together. The talking and exchanging and remembering lasted for hours.

After the reunion, the documentary crew interviewed men from both sides. Many described this experience as the most healing thing they had ever experienced. Some of them were overcome with emotion, wondering how the hatred and anger was ripped out of their hearts as they hugged their former adversaries. This time they had seen them as human beings, not enemies. They had more in common than all the differences that had separated them in wartime.

A supreme example of national forgiveness is found in the events that followed World War II. For six long years, the United States and its allies had battled two powerful enemies who used the devastating weapons of modern industrial warfare to conquer most of Europe, a sizable part of east Asia, and all of the western Pacific island nations and territories.

Nazi Germany, in addition to mercilessly fighting its adversaries, also undertook the inhumane and unfathomable task of exterminating as many European Jews as they could, making this almost as much of a priority as waging war against the United States and the Allied nations. Dissenters from dictatorial Nazi rule in the occupied countries were also sent to concentration camps, where they served as slaves or worse, many of them dying from starvation, disease, or overwork.

The Japanese, completely ignoring the Geneva Conventions, starved their American and Allied prisoners of war and often used them as slave laborers in mines and on construction projects.

While these wartime atrocities were addressed and judgment rendered in the Nuremburg trials of Nazi leaders and similar judicial proceedings against Japanese military leaders, human nature would normally have led the victorious Allied nations to take economic revenge against their enemies. After the First World War, the victors had demanded and extracted large monetary reparations from defeated Germany and Austria, a punishment that impoverished both nations in the years to follow. Those very onerous reparations contributed to the eventual rise of Adolf Hitler and ultimately to a resumption of the First World War in the even more disastrous Second World War.

America had emerged from World War II as the most powerful nation on earth. With only seven percent of the world's population, the United States had 42 percent of its income and half of the world's manufacturing capacity, according to statistics quoted in Paul Johnson's

A History of the American People. America produced 62 percent of the world's oil and owned three quarters of the world's gold, making it by far the wealthiest nation on earth. During the war, its vast production capabilities had made the difference between victory and defeat on almost every front, with tanks, trucks, aircraft, food, guns, ammunition, and other wartime necessities supplied to the Allies without charge.

While the natural response in victory might have demanded reparations from Germany and Japan and repayment from Britain and Russia for America's wartime largesse, President Harry S. Truman and American leaders chose not to do so. Instead, they chose to use American wealth and productive capacity to rebuild the economies and feed the citizens of its former enemies. Unveiled in 1947 and named for then Secretary of State George Marshall, the Marshall Plan funneled American food, technology, products, and assistance to Germany, formerly occupied France, and Italy. Japan, although occupied by American troops in the years immediately following the war, was allowed to keep its traditions and governmental structure. A new constitution brought Japan into the modern world and restricted it from having offensive military forces. The Allied countries provided aid to rebuild Japanese industries, cities, and infrastructure. Within ten years of implementing these vast aid programs, America's former enemies had become friends and partners in building a new and hopeful postwar world.

Such an undertaking is not to be found anywhere else in earth's long history of warfare and conflict. For a country to fight, as the Americans did, a long and brutal war, losing more than four hundred thousand soldiers, sailors, and airmen, and with more than a million wounded, we might expect a lingering degree of hatred for those who perpetrated earth's most disastrous war. In the case of this, the most extensive and destructive conflict the world has ever known, it was almost as though Americans—both leaders and, for the most part, citizens—decided that these former enemies needed to be forgiven; it was time to move on to a more promising future.

The Marshall Plan in Europe and the American effort in rebuilding Japan also had political and economic motivations. The United States needed healthy trading partners in the postwar era; we needed to have a renewed Germany and Japan as allies in the "Cold War" against Soviet Russia that began soon after the war ended. But the decision by the United States to rebuild its former enemies and the willingness of Americans to help them reconstruct their nations qualify as one of the great moments in American history. Because of the willingness to forgive, America put a dreadful conflict behind as it began the world leadership role it has had in the subsequent half century.

THE LIBERATION: Key Principles to Remember

The United States Marines at Iwo Jima taught us . . .

WE NEED TO FORGIVE, BUT WE SHOULD NOT FORGET

- Although taking offense at the actions and words of others happens easily in normal situations, difficult times sharpen our emotions and bring our feelings to the surface, making it more difficult to withstand being offended.
- When we are harmed, we need to seek realistic resolutions to that harm. But holding on to the anger and hurt usually hurts us most.
- As we forgive, we learn to work with the weaknesses of others. By remembering, we maintain the vigilance necessary to avoid future harm. When Washington reminded us that "Vigilance is the price of Liberty," he was not saying we should never forgive others, but that we can forgive and, in remembering, protect ourselves and our future.

NOTES

1. James E. Faust, "The Healing Power of Forgiveness," *Ensign*, May 2007, 68.
2. Stephen E. Ambrose, *American Heritage New History of World War II* (New York: Viking, 1997), 563.
3. Ibid., 565–66.

Epilogue

THE LIGHT

THE LIGHT WILL COME

This book has shown examples of confronting and conquering challenging times, both in our nation and in our individual lives. In reviewing examples of how great men and women have encountered and overcome challenges, we have discussed practical things we can do to channel our fears, torment, and anguish in positive and productive ways. But there still may be days and even weeks and months when the burden seems almost too great to bear and when finding the energy to survive, never mind thrive, is almost more than we can do. When we have nothing more to give, when we have no energy to push forward, we must at least "hold on, for the light will come."[1]

When I was a young boy, my grandfather would take us to Timpanogos Cave in the Wasatch Mountains of northern Utah. I was fascinated with the cave, which ages ago had been dissolved out of the limestone rock layers by underground water in the bowels of Mount Timpanogos, one of the highest peaks in the range. The cave's slimy, dripping stalactites and water-splashed stalagmites took many fanciful shapes, and despite the long and steep climb to the cave entrance, I visited it many times—never tiring of the experience.

My greatest memory of these visits is rooted in a particular moment in every tour when we would arrive at a great open space with tumbled slabs of rock on the floor and an arched ceiling overhead. The ranger leading the tour would have us all stand very still and would then turn off the lights in the cave, plunging us into total blackness. After a few very disorienting moments of total darkness, he would strike a match. Like a fox in a henhouse, my eyes would laser in on that tiny speck of light in the smothering layer of blackness. I don't know if God or Charles Darwin was at work, but my mind and my eyes instinctively knew to search and hold onto even the tiniest speck of light in all that inky blackness.

And so it must be with us in our moments of greatest challenge. We must focus our minds and our eyes on the tiniest bit of light in the nightshade of our momentary experience. And, having found that tiny spark of hope (either in remembrance or in future expectation) we must hold on—and wait and hope for it to grow.

THE PAIN OF AN EMANCIPATION NOT ANTICIPATED

Abraham Lincoln, sixteenth President of the United States, faced his share of dark times during the American Civil War. And in much of that gloomy and uncertain period in our history, Lincoln had to find his way alone. In part, this isolation stemmed from including political rivals in several key positions in his administration. Because some of them possessed egos telling them they were superior in ability and knowledge to this "outsider" President, Lincoln spent much energy in keeping together a working coalition among this politically diverse group. In 1861, relatively few of Lincoln's cabinet and other advisors thought the new President was up to the job.

He also faced other daunting problems. Before Abraham Lincoln even took the oath of office, seven southern states had seceded from the United States and formed a government they called the Confederate States of America. They also seized control of forts and other federal properties in the South. After assuming office, Lincoln was powerless to stop additional southern states from leaving the Union, including Virginia, whose boundaries included the west bank of the Potomac, just across the river from the federal capital, Washington, DC.

Some attempts at reconciliation were tried, but after Confederate troops attacked and captured Fort Sumter in South Carolina, the two sides took up arms against each other. Early military actions all seemed to favor the Confederacy. The first major battle, at Bull Run, only twenty-five miles southwest of Washington in Virginia, turned into a rout of the Union forces. Expecting an easy Union victory, the wealthy elite of Washington drove out in their carriages to have a summer picnic and watch the battle, as though it was a theatrical performance. They ended up fleeing back to the capital, clogging the roads along with the retreating Army of the Potomac.

Other military and political challenges confronted Lincoln during the remainder of 1861, with the Commander in Chief searching for a general who could lead the Union armies to victory. Union and Confederate forces alternately advanced and retreated through a series of battles in Virginia, western Maryland, and southern Pennsylvania that continued until Union forces defeated Confederate General Robert E. Lee and his armies in a decisive battle at Gettysburg, Pennsylvania, in July of 1863.

At the beginning of 1862, the tide of battle turned slightly in the Union's favor, especially in Tennessee, where General Ulysses S. Grant was emerging as the most effective and successful of Lincoln's field commanders.

For a few brief months, these were heady and buoying times, not just for Abraham Lincoln's administration and the military, but also for his wife, Mary Todd Lincoln. On February 5, the Lincolns threw a large and lavish party to celebrate their recent renovation of the White House. Five hundred guests attended the affair, numbering among them generals, cabinet members, diplomats, Supreme Court justices, and others of the elite Washington establishment. After dancing and socializing, they enjoyed a midnight buffet dinner supplied by New York's most famous and expensive caterer. The party went on until dawn.

The euphoria of the military victories and the superlative White House party did not last long for the Lincolns, who soon found themselves dealing with a very personal tragedy. As summarized by Lincoln historian David Herbert Donald in his authoritative biography *Lincoln*:

> Shortly before the party their son Willie had fallen ill with "bilious fever"—probably typhoid fever, caused by pollution in the White House water system. Deeply anxious, his parents considered canceling the grand reception, but the family doctor assured them that the boy was in no immediate danger. During the next two weeks. . . . Willie grew worse and worse.
>
> Sitting up with his sick children [his younger son Tad also contracted the same illness] night after night, Lincoln was able to transact little business, and he seemed to stumble through his duties. . . . During the two weeks after the grand party [Willie] grew weaker and weaker, and Lincoln began to despair of his recovery. On February 20 the end came. Stepping into his office, Lincoln said in a voice choked with emotion [to his secretary, John G. Nicolay]: "Well, Nicolay, my boy is gone—he is actually gone!"[2]

Willie's death had a profound effect on Abraham Lincoln. Seeing the lifeless face of his eleven-year-old son, Lincoln was reported to have said, "My poor boy. He was too good for this earth. God has called him home. I know that he is much better off in heaven, but then we loved him so. It is hard, hard to have him die!" Mary Todd Lincoln could not bring herself to attend the funeral, which was held in the White House, and she took to her bed for three weeks following his death. Tad, the younger son, survived his illness but for some time was heartbroken over the death of the older brother he loved.

The grief-stricken President turned to religion for solace, as well as the writings of Shakespeare and others. David Herbert Donald reports:

> On a trip to Fort Monroe long after Willie was buried, Lincoln read passages from Macbeth and King Lear aloud to an aide, and then from King John he recited Constance's lament for her son:
>
> 'And, father cardinal, I have heard you say
> That we shall see and know our friends in heaven:
> If that be true, I shall see my boy again.'
>
> His voice trembled and he wept.[3]

And so, in a deeply poignant and personal moment, an emancipation neither anticipated nor desired by the person who would come to be known as The Great Emancipator, had come to pass, and his beloved Willie was gone.

It has been written: "For he [God] maketh his sun to rise on the evil and on the good, and sendeth rain on the just and on the unjust" (Matthew 5:45).

As it was with Abraham Lincoln, so it will be with us—rain, undesired and often undeserved, will come into our lives. The clouds will gather, the sky will blacken, and the storms will come. All we can do some days is just hold on and wait for the light.

A SMUDGE ON THE HORIZON, A SHADOW ON THE WATER

Another metaphor about holding on and exercising hope and courage in overcoming life's challenges is found in an incident attributed in the 1998 motion picture *Elizabeth* to Sir Walter Raleigh, one of the earliest of the English explorers involved in the settlement of America. Raleigh, perhaps best known for having thrown his cloak over a puddle in the path of Queen Elizabeth I, is shown in the movie performing that chivalrous but historically questionable deed. As the motion picture continues, Raleigh develops a close and personal friendship with Her Majesty as he seeks her financial support for his tiny colony in the New World. Elizabeth seems to enjoy hearing him tell of his voyages and the new American colony he has named for her, the Virgin Queen—Virginia.

After speaking of the terrors and uncertainties of crossing the wide Atlantic on his voyage to Virginia, the actor playing Raleigh (who at this point was not yet Sir Walter) describes his arrival in the New World:

> At first it's no more than a haze on the horizon, the ghost of a haze, the pure line corrupted. But clouds do that, and storms. So you watch, you watch. Then it's a smudge, a shadow on the far water. For a day, for another day, the stain slowly spreads along the horizon, and takes form—until on the third day you let yourself believe. You dare to whisper the word—land! Land. Life, Resurrection . . . coming out of the vast unknown, out of the immensity, into safe harbour at last.

For Walter Raleigh, his long-desired goal appeared first as a smudge on the horizon. So too, our own lives may at times seem buried in the depths of challenge, our goals out of reach and uncertain of fulfillment. Light rarely bursts over us in the way of solution or salvation when we are in the midst of our greatest fights. But if we are watching, the light may initially appear only as a "smudge" of hope. If we will keep looking for it (like I as a boy would look for the struck match in pitch-black Timpanogos Cave) and then hold on, it will grow and gradually define its own form of rescue and salvation.

My hope for this simple book is that it might be a smudge on the far horizon, especially for those of you who despair. And so, if anything I have said thus far is helpful, I have fulfilled my desire. Use that which has benefit for you, and forgive me my possible arrogance in prescribing the rest. Where you find use or usefulness, share with others, for in words often attributed to John F. Kennedy: "A rising tide lifts all boats"—if we will allow it to do so.

One final thought: In his book *Inventing a Nation*, author Gore Vidal recalls a conversation he had with the young President John F.

Kennedy in 1961, while visiting the Kennedy compound at Hyannisport, Massachusetts.

The conversation went like this:

> **President Kennedy:**
>
> [A mutual friend and relation] spent his life collecting Horace Walpole. He said to me, the other day, about the eighteenth century, his specialty . . . how do you explain how a sort of backwoods country like this, with only three million people, could have produced the three great geniuses of the eighteenth century—Franklin, Jefferson and Hamilton?
>
> **Gore Vidal:**
>
> Time. They had more of it, they stayed home on the farm in winter. They read. Wrote letters. Apparently thought, something no longer done—in public life.
>
> **President Kennedy:**
>
> You know, in this . . . job . . . I get to meet everybody—all these great movers and shakers, and the thing I am most struck by the lot of them, is how second-rate they are. Then, you read all those debates over the Constitution. . . . Nothing like that now. Nothing.[4]

I don't know that we would all qualify as "second-rate," but I do believe we have much to learn from those who founded this nation and brought it through its worst times. We could all benefit, myself included, from taking a little more time, reading more, staying home a little more, writing, talking, and most of all, thinking—about many things, including perhaps the lessons we can learn from those who have made this land "the home of the brave."

In closing, let me leave a final and simple prayer, beloved of our Pilgrim forebears, from the book of Ecclesiasticus, 44, ca. 180 BC:

> Let us now praise famous men and our fathers that begat us. . . .
>
> All these were honored in their generation, and were the glory of their times.

God bless our nation, the United States of America. God bless our founding mothers and fathers. And God bless you and your house and the houses of all those you call your own.

EPILOGUE: Key Principles to Remember

President Abraham Lincoln taught us . . .

IF ALL YOU CAN DO IS HOLD ON, THEN HOLD ON—

FOR THE LIGHT OF BETTER TIMES WILL ALWAYS COME.

- There are few people in our nation's history who were more engaged, hardworking, passionate and brave in the defense of the nation's freedom than was Abraham Lincoln. But even someone of his character had a breaking point and, with the death of his young son, he had nothing more to give. And so, he just held on and with the help of family and friends, kept going and kept leading us through some of America's darkest hours. Having seen the war through to its completion, Lincoln's brave life was snuffed out by an assassin's bullet.

NOTES

1. Michael McLean, "Hold On."
2. David Herbert Donald, *Lincoln* (New York: Simon & Schuster, 1995), 336.
3. Ibid.
4. Gore Vidal, *Inventing a Nation: Washington, Adams, Jefferson* (New Haven, CT: Yale University Press, 2003), 187–88

Appendix

APPLICATION TO AMERICA'S YOUTH

These questions are provided with two ends in mind:

1. If I was young again, I could have learned life's lessons earlier by thinking about some of the ideas below. As a young person, with all your goals, potential, and aspirations—read these questions, think about them, and, where appropriate, make real changes early in your life.
2. As a parent, consider these questions, in concert with reading this book with your children, as a framework for discussion as you complete each chapter.

PROLOGUE: "THE HOME OF THE BRAVE"

- Think about challenging times in your life. Where did you go or what did you do to become more "brave"?
- How do you initially respond to a difficult or frightening situation? Are you OK with this response? Have you learned different, and perhaps better, ways to respond? Where could you go to learn new and better ways to act in challenging situations?
- If you could change one thing about yourself in the area of "bravery," what would that one thing be?

PREFACE: WE HAVE PASSED THIS WAY BEFORE

- Who are the "great oaks" in your life (the older, more experienced, trustworthy and reliable people)?
- Do you have the kind of relationships you desire to have with these people? Could you go to them in a time of challenge or difficulty and get their advice or help? What could you do to improve your relationship with them?
- Who are your heroes or models in life? Do you know enough about their lives and their ideas and actions to learn from them? Can you build on what they knew and learn to become a better person (can you stand on the shoulders of these giants)?

CHAPTER I: THE LEGACY

- The Pilgrims were "pragmatic," which means they took the situation as it was (not the way they wanted it to be) and looked for simple and practical solutions. Are you pragmatic—especially in challenging situations? Or are you a "woulda, coulda, shoulda" person, trying to avoid the reality as long as possible? Are you a practical person in difficult situations or do you tend to lose too much control to emotion and fear? What, if anything, could you do differently?
- Difficult situations can be threatening. Sometimes being threatened does not bring out our best characteristics. Are you or can you be kind in difficult situations, like Abigail Adams? Or do you sometimes let out your less attractive characteristics and regret it later? Could you learn to be more kind, even when your day is not going well?
- When things are tough for you, can you, like General Washington, put at least some of your own needs aside to do kind or

helpful things for others who are suffering as well? What could you improve in this area?

CHAPTER II: THE LENS

- Do you look for the positive or the opportunity (can you see the flag through the "rocket's red glare, the bombs bursting in air")? Or do you struggle to see anything positive in difficult situations? How does what you see or focus on affect how you feel? When things are difficult, do you struggle to find the strength to get out of bed, to find a solution, to get going, to hang in there?
- What do your "patterns of behavior" tell you about the principles/beliefs on your Belief Window? (Remember—your beliefs show up in your behavior.) Are there principles/beliefs on your Belief Window that are not meeting your needs over time?
- Sometimes difficult times in our lives can feel like "Dobermans." How do you respond to the Dobermans in your life? Is this the way you want to respond? What, if anything, would you like to change on your Belief Window that would make your response to the challenges in your life more like you would want it to be?
- Are there principles that others have espoused (like General MacArthur) that you would like on your Belief Window—such as duty, honor, modesty, and strength? What might those principles be? Make a list, carry it with you, and look at it regularly—especially in situations where you may not be at your best—and remind yourself of who you want to be and how you want to act.

CHAPTER III: THE LAW

- Can you make what you have available to you work for you, especially in difficult times (like Captain Barry with his "washtubs"), or are you always waiting for or complaining about not having what you need to escape the problem, to do better, to achieve your goals? Is this ability to make do with simple things something you would like to acquire? Who do you know who lives this way and could teach you how to "make do"?
- Are you doing the things in your life (diet, exercise, adequate sleep, avoiding addictive substances or activities, living your values, building emotional and spiritual resilience) that create the energy you need in your life—especially in challenging times?
- What habits or activities are interfering with your ability to generate and maintain the energy you need and desire? What will you do to make the changes necessary?
- Are you channeling your energy into the paths you desire? Are you spending your hard-won strength well and on the things you care about, or is it being wasted or sucked up in activities or habits you don't value?

CHAPTER IV: THE LANDSCAPE

- Have you ever thought about and can you identify the "no control" events that regularly occur in your life?
- Are you an "adapter" or a "complainer"? Do you want to change?
- Have you ever thought about and can you identify the "some control" events that regularly occur in your life?

- Are you an "influencer" in your relationships or are you a "manipulator"? Are your approaches to your relationships working for you or could you do better?
- Have you ever thought about and can you identify the "total control" events that regularly occur in your life?
- Are you an "actor" and a "doer" or are you a "procrastinator"? If you do procrastinate, what is one thing you would like to stop putting off (homework, assignments or chores, apologizing for mistakes)?
- Can you use these techniques (adapt, influence, and act) in your everyday life to make more good choices than bad throughout the day—like General Eisenhower?

CHAPTER V: THE LION

- What are the "lions"—the really big challenges in your life? Do these challenges frighten or overwhelm you so much you don't know what to do? Can you find even a small place to start? If not, who do you trust enough to ask for help in starting to deal with these "lions" in your life?
- Do you have even a tiny piece of the courage Sergeant Bain showed? Can you accept yourself as you are—with both strengths and weaknesses? Or do you dwell on your limitations? How do you keep your morale high when your weaknesses challenge your goals? How could you "accentuate the positives" in your life more? Do you have the friends and associates who emphasize what is good about you, or do they tend to put you down because of your weaknesses?
- What can you learn from Dr. King's great strength in the middle of huge challenges? Can you be as selfless as he was and put your own comfort aside to help others? How often do you serve others, and what have those experiences taught you?

- Have you learned, after it was over, that a difficult situation was actually an opportunity or a blessing that, although really difficult while it was happening, ended up being a real help to you?

CHAPTER VI: THE LEVERAGE

- Are you good at living with and working with others? Or do other people cause you stress and frustration? Are you part of the problem? Do you sometimes act to manipulate others inappropriately in order to get your own way? Has this hurt your relationships with people you care about? Has it hurt people you maybe don't care that much for? Is this the type of person you want to be?
- When a person isn't open to your ideas, your suggestions, or your approach, can you "agree to disagree agreeably" or do you lash out, criticize, or even end relationships that aren't going exactly your way? Will this meet your needs over time?
- Is there a person in your life who, because you acted too aggressively or tried to manipulate them, is no longer a friend? Would you be willing to adapt a little, apologize, and repair that friendship?

CHAPTER VII: THE LEADER

- Have you ever procrastinated or put something off that you later regretted not acting on (remember the emerald ring story)? Do you have the courage to act on things that frighten you?
- As long as your actions are moral and ethical, are you prepared to take some flak from others for doing what you know to be right even though it's not popular? Are you prepared to "stand

for something" that is not currently popular or trendy? If you have done this, was the short-term pain worth the long-term gain in knowing that you were able to do what was right?

CHAPTER VIII: THE LIBERATION

- Has someone ever hurt you so badly you believed, at least at the time, you could never forgive them? Have things changed since then? Has the pain lessened or at least become more bearable? Has a small window for forgiveness opened up?
- Have you ever forgiven someone for something harmful they have done to you? How did you feel? Is this a feeling you would like to have again? Have you ever experienced being forgiven by someone you have hurt? Would you like people to be forgiving of you when you make mistakes, intentional or otherwise?
- Can you think of someone you could forgive today? What is one simple thing you might do or say to forgive this person? As you are contemplating an act of forgiveness, you may struggle with letting go of legitimate feelings of pain and harm. Can you let go and allow the healing of forgiveness to resolve the situation?

EPILOGUE: THE LIGHT

- Have you experienced moments of great challenge where you were worried if you could hold on "for the light to come"? How did you gain that strength? Did you have family or friends who helped you through? Did you have models or mentors to follow? Did prayer, meditation, or other spiritual activity help and strengthen you? Does music, reading, physical activity, or a change of scenery help you when you are really struggling?

- What are the "specks of light" in your dark moments? Do you know where to find them when you need them?
- Whatever your source of strength, do you keep it close at hand and have you learned to use it as your strength?
- Are you reading, studying, pondering, and talking about great ideas and concepts? Or do you, as President Kennedy said, do things that may push you closer to a "second-rate" rather than a "first-rate" mind?
- Did you learn enough interesting and helpful things from history in this book to make more of an effort to read, understand, talk about, and learn from the history we all share—the history of "famous men and women and the fathers and mothers that begat us?"
- Do you really understand how blessed your life is just by having the opportunity to live in this great country—the United States of America?

SELECTED BIBLIOGRAPHY

Ambrose, Stephen E. *American Heritage New History of World War II.* New York: Viking, 1997.

———. *The Supreme Commander: The War Years of General Dwight D. Eisenhower.* New York: Doubleday, and Jackson, MS: University Press of Mississippi, 1970.

Beschloss, Michael. *Presidential Courage: Brave Leaders and How They Changed America.* New York: Simon & Schuster, 2007.

Donald, David Herbert. *Lincoln.* New York: Simon & Schuster, 1995.

Carson, Clayborne, Ed. *The Autobiography of Martin Luther King, Jr.* New York: Warner Books, 1998.

Goodwin, Doris Kearns. *Team of Rivals: The Political Genius of Abraham Lincoln.* New York: Simon & Schuster, 2005.

Griffin, Martin I. J. *The Story of Commodore John Barry.* Philadelphia: Publisher unknown, 1908.

Kennedy, Robert F. *Thirteen Days: A Memoir of the Cuban Missile Crisis.* New York: W.W. Norton & Company, 1971.

Johnson, Paul. *A History of the American People.* New York: HarperCollins, 1998.

McCullough, David. *1776.* New York: Simon & Schuster, 2005.

———. *John Adams.* New York: Simon & Schuster, 2001.

Philbrick, Nathaniel. *Mayflower: A Story of Courage, Community, and War.* New York: Viking, 2006.

Vidal, Gore. *Inventing a Nation: Washington, Adams, Jefferson.* New Haven, CT: Yale University Press, 2003.

ABOUT THE AUTHORS

Richard L. Godfrey is a cofounder of The Galileo Initiative. Prior to the launch of The Galileo Initiative, Richard worked as a senior international consultant with Franklin Covey, where he was recognized as The Consultant with Greatest Value to Clients. Over more than two decades, Richard has worked with corporate, government, military, and not-for-profit organization clients all around the globe. He has specialized in adapting leadership and productivity concepts to the specific needs of his clients and audiences and is highly sought after as a keynote speaker, training facilitator, and management consultant.

In addition to being the lead author of *On the Shoulders of Giants: Learning Leadership Skills from Great Americans*, Richard is lead author of *The Seven Laws of Learning: Why Great Leaders Are Also Great Teachers*. He recently finished his latest book, *The Insulated Generation: How to Save Your Children from a World Gone Mad*. He is also working on his first novel, *The Sixth Tablet*, and has aided Curtis Hill on his recent book *Customer Service DNA*. In addition to his books, Richard has developed over a dozen leadership development and personal productivity training courses taught around the globe.

Hyrum W. Smith is the principal founder of The Galileo Initiative and former Vice-Chairman of the Board of Franklin Covey. Hyrum is a highly sought after keynote speaker and author. For nearly three decades, he has been motivating people to see reality more clearly and to gain better control of their personal and professional lives. Hyrum's speeches and presentations have been acclaimed by American and international audiences.

Hyrum is the author of several nationally published and acclaimed books, including *The 10 Natural Laws of Successful Time and Life Management*, *What Matters Most*, *The Advanced Day Planner User's Guide*, and *The Modern Gladiator*, and is coauthor of *The Seven Laws of Learning* (with Richard L. Godfrey and Gerreld L. Pulsipher), *Pain Is Inevitable; Misery Is Optional* (with Gerreld L. Pulsipher), and *Excellence through Time Management* (with Richard Winwood).

Gerreld L. Pulsipher is a cofounder of The Galileo Initiative. With a dual degree in journalism and fine arts, he blends extensive experience in writing, graphic design, and curriculum design with a lifelong interest in history and natural history. His focus in The Galileo Initiative has been on designing training curriculum materials and publications. He was also instrumental in developing the teaching and learning process that forms the underpinning of *The Seven Laws of Learning.*

Jerry is the coauthor of several books, including *Gaining Control: Your Key to Freedom and Success* (with Robert F. Bennett and Kurt Hanks), *Five Secrets to Personal Productivity* (with Kurt Hanks and David Pulsipher), *Getting Your Message Across* (with Kurt Hanks), *Tourism: The Good, The Bad, and the Ugly* (with John E. Rosenow), *Pain Is Inevitable; Misery Is Optional* (with Hyrum W. Smith), and *The Seven Laws of Learning: Why Great Leaders Are Also Great Teachers* (with Richard L. Godfrey and Hyrum W. Smith).

0 26575 59261 0